Domestic Life in Wales

Domestic Life in Wales

S. Minwel Tibbott

EDITED BY BETH THOMAS

University of Wales Press
National Museums & Galleries of Wales
Cardiff

2002

British Library Cataloguing in Publication Data
A catalogue record for this book is available from the British Library.

ISBN   0-7083-1746-4

Typeset at the University of Wales Press
Printed in Great Britain by Gwasg Gomer, Llandysul

Contents

Preface

Before her untimely death in 1998, Minwel Tibbott had already begun editing articles previously published in various journals with a view to presentation in a single volume. It is my privilege to be able to fulfil a debt to Minwel, a friend and mentor, by bringing the project to fruition.

The articles reproduced here were written over a period from 1974 to 1995 (see bibliography on pp. xvi–xvii). Inevitably there have been many changes during this period, for example the reorganization of county boundaries, and Minwel would doubtless have incorporated these into the revised text. However, in order to avoid confusion and preserve as much as possible of her original work, we have tried to keep such alterations to a minimum.

We are indebted to many people for contributing to this volume, not least the many women interviewed by the author over the years, and those who have donated or allowed us to reproduce many of the photographs used as illustrations. Any rights that may exist in this material are acknowledged. Thanks are also due to the Society for Folk Life Studies and the British Association for Local History for their permission to publish material which first appeared in their journals. Finally I would like to thank Delwyn Tibbott for his assistance with the proofs and Trefor M. Owen for honouring his promise to Minwel to write the foreword.

Beth Thomas
Keeper, Social and Cultural History
Museum of Welsh Life

Minwel Tibbott on recording fieldwork in Pentyrch, 1970.

Foreword

When Minwel Tibbott asked me if I would contribute a foreword to the volume of articles on folk life which she was preparing for publication, I readily agreed. As her colleague in the Welsh Folk Museum (now the Museum of Welsh Life), St Fagans, I had followed the development of her research and had admired her ability to combine the use of oral sources with literary and documentary evidence in her field of study. Her sudden death in October 1998, shortly after our conversation, however, cast a deep shadow over what would otherwise have been both a source of great pleasure and an opportunity to express to her personally my appreciation of her contribution to the work of the Museum during my term as Curator.

Sara Minwel Williams was born in Nantgwynau, Llansawel, Carmarthenshire, and brought up in Crug-y-bar nearby, in Felin Newydd, then a farm and working corn mill. She graduated in Welsh at the University College of Wales, as it then was, in Aberystwyth, and proceeded to undertake research. Her MA dissertation, submitted in 1959 and published in part in 1969, dealt with the sixteenth-century medical treatise *Castell yr Iechyd,* a translation of Sir Thomas Elyot's 'Castel of Helthe' by the colourful copyist, chronicler and soldier, Elis Gruffydd 'of Calais'. She married a fellow researcher, Delwyn Tibbott, who had been engaged in a parallel study of Elis Gruffydd's *Llysieuwr* (herbal), and it is he, who was also a member of the staff of the Welsh Folk Museum, who has actively encouraged the publication of the present volume.

Minwel Tibbott joined the staff of the Welsh Folk Museum in 1969 as a Research Assistant in the Department of Oral Traditions and Dialects and later became an Assistant Keeper. In a Welsh article published in the journal *Barn* in February 1971 she set out her aims and reported on her progress after fifteen months in post. She tells us she had been gathering information about the preparation and cooking of food in various parts of Wales but that this was only the beginning of a project which would eventually involve devoting her attention to other tasks traditionally carried out by women, such as sewing, knitting and quilting. The prime source of this oral evidence was to be the oldest generation among the people of Wales. Although this meant, naturally, that she would rely mainly on the information gleaned from women, she added that it would be useful to have the observations of the menfolk on the food prepared for them. As the articles included in this volume testify, she achieved a number of these aims and deserves to be recognized as a pioneer in the field of women's studies in Wales.

In her fieldwork during these early months she had devoted herself to the study of foods, only later taking up the other topics related to women's work. The medicinal qualities of various foods which she mentions in her article was a subject to be shared with (and later handed over to) another research assistant, Ann Elizabeth Williams, who concentrated on the recording and study of folk medicine. Already in 1971 Minwel Tibbott had seen some interesting patterns emerging. She had begun with the study of the preparation of that most traditional of Welsh foods, oatcakes, and had found that there were regional variations both in the techniques used and in the terminology employed. This research was to form the basis of her article on 'Traditional Breads of Wales' which also included a discussion of various types of ovens and communal bakehouses. A further article on 'Cheese-making in Glamorgan', also reproduced in this volume, exemplifies her interest in regional traditions and with the differences to be found even within the same county. In it she begins with a description of the methods divulged to her by an octogenarian informant in the fertile northern part of the Vale of Glamorgan, known as the Border Vale – the third generation in her family to have been taught the skills of a dairy maid. She then proceeds to compare the methods employed in making the well-known Caerphilly cheese produced on the hill farms and sold in the town of that name to the growing mining population of the nineteenth century. Two books by her, published by the Museum, reveal her continuing concern to record local variations. The first, *Amser Bwyd*, appeared in 1974, followed by an English version, *Welsh Fare*, in 1976. This was an illustrated collection of traditional food recipes and cooking methods from all parts of Wales. Over eighty informants, mostly women, who had contributed to this work were thanked by her in the preface to the volume. The recipes she printed were eagerly tried out, and some of her informants were persuaded to give demonstrations to visitors to the Museum. The second work was *Geirfa'r Gegin*, published in 1983, a comprehensive Welsh glossary of various kinds of foods, cooking methods and utensils, with their English equivalents, and illustrated with forty-four line-drawings of utensils. Although the material culture of the hearth and its cooking implements had been studied previously, notably by Dr Iorwerth Peate in an article on the baking pot and by Dr Eurwyn Wiliam in an article on the architectural development of the hearth, the actual preparation of food using such implements on the hearth was hitherto a neglected topic.

Minwel Tibbott's interest extended beyond the actual cooking methods to the social context of food and diet. She had already identified as topics for research in her 1971 article meals associated with special working occasions on the farm such as threshing, peat-cutting and harvesting. There were also the festive celebrations, such as Christmas Day and New Year's Day, christenings and weddings on which special foods were served. Her subsequent work on these themes bore fruit in the article on 'Liberality and hospitality: food as communication in Wales' included here. The broad subject of diet, however, unlike that of the archaeology of the hearth, had attracted the attention of antiquarians and social historians. Early in the twentieth century the two authors of a volume dealing with the social history of Wales had discussed the fare of the countryman using material collected by the Royal Commission on Land in Wales set up in 1893. Both authors, Sir John Rhŷs, the eminent Celtic scholar, and Sir D. Brynmor Jones, a prominent legal figure and Member of Parliament, had served on the Commission and had in fact previously drafted the sections used by them in their book and submitted them to their fellow Commissioners. Minwel Tibbott, too, in an article on 'Traditional foods in Wales at the beginning of the twentieth century', not included here, drawing on oral evidence, similarly discusses the diet of the farming community in terms of the food eaten at the various meals of the day, before going on to deal with other topics discussed at greater length in the articles reproduced in this volume. Some of the findings of the nineteenth-century Commissioners, incidentally, make interesting reading. One witness appearing before the Commission at Bala, Merioneth, described the fare of the hill farmer which had not changed very much since his childhood, in the following words:

> First of all we had in the morning bruised oatmeal cake and butter-milk; then we had some bread-and-butter and tea. For dinner we had bacon and potatoes. For tea, at about three or four o'clock, we used to have a lot of *sucan*, followed by a cup of tea. *Sucan* is a kind of thin flummery, or something like that. Then we had porridge or bread-and-cheese with butter-milk for supper.

This basic fare survived well into the twentieth century, as Minwel Tibbott's articles show, and a contemporary social anthropologist writing in 1964 compared the diet of the people of Llanfrothen in the same county of Merioneth unfavourably with both the working-class diet described by Richard Hoggart in the Leeds district and the fare she remembered as a child in London. 'The beef-dripping for breakfast and celery and radishes for tea, which every working-class Londoner knows never appear on Llan tables. The diet is poor and monotonous and is relieved only by "tins for visitors".' As to social differences in diet in the late nineteenth century, the evidence is conflicting. The report, for example, comments upon the absence of any marked differences between tenant farmers and small freeholders and between small farmers and farm labourers in respect of their diet. However, the evidence contained in the *Report of the Royal Commission on the Agricultural Labourer in Wales*, published in 1894 strongly suggests that farm labourers were given inferior food in some areas. In the Vale of Clwyd, for example, some labourers who bought butter from their employers found the reputedly pure butter had been mixed with 'butterine' bought from the local shop, and that second-class grain had been used to make the bread fed to servants at their table. Fatty bacon with hardly any 'red' in it was often cooked for them by the youngest and most inexperienced maidservant. Furthermore, because information from various parts of Wales had been gathered in the preparation of these two reports it was now becoming possible to investigate regional differences. Rhŷs and Jones point out that, in the opinion of one witness, Merioneth folk ate more oatmeal and porridge than did the inhabitants of the Vale of Clwyd and that the food eaten in Merioneth was better. The more prosperous border counties fared better than other parts, for instance Cardiganshire where meat broth or *cawl* was the staple dish. The developing industrial areas also appeared to enjoy a better diet then the farming districts, and tea was becoming the standard beverage throughout Wales.

The purpose of the Royal Commissions, so characteristic of the nineteenth century, was the investigation of social conditions in a period of change following industrialization, but their documentation of contemporary diets (and other features such as housing and labour conditions) was not pursued on academic lines. Nevertheless, the information assembled in this way assumes considerable importance in the absence of many other contemporary sources.

One of these sources, if erratic and sometimes superficial, was the literature, published and unpublished, of the tourists who visited Wales during the eighteenth century and well into the Victorian age and who wrote in their journals, letters and books about what they had seen. Their ignorance of the Welsh language and their patronizing attitudes frequently misled them, and their experience of food was often confined to the local hostelry. However, the more perceptive and reliable among them, such as Thomas Pennant (1726–98), and Benjamin Heath Malkin (1789–1842), whose evidence Minwel Tibbott uses, provide valuable eyewitness accounts of conditions which they encountered on their journeys on horseback through the countryside. Others, such as the scientist Alfred Russel Wallace, who were not strictly tourists but were imbued with intellectual curiosity, left valuable accounts of everyday conditions, including food in those districts where they had briefly stayed. Yet others, like T. J. Llewelyn Prichard, who wrote in English for a predominantly Welsh readership, sometimes described for the benefit of their readers what might be regarded as exotic in other parts of Wales. Prichard's volume of poetry, *Cambrian Minstrelsy*, published in 1823, for example, records the making of laver (*llafan* or 'black butter'), a local speciality, near St David's, Pembrokeshire, describing how the seaweed was gathered in spring: 'having washed it clean they lay it to sweeten between two flat stones, then shred it small and knead it well, like dough for bread; and afterwards make it up into great balls or rolls which some eat raw, and others, fry with oatmeal'. In an earlier period the correspondence of the Morris brothers is often valuable in this respect, especially when Lewis Morris (1700–65), having moved from his native Anglesey to Cardiganshire, refers in his letters to his brothers William and Richard, to the different social conditions which he has encountered in his adopted county, including the food he misses so much. Minwel Tibbott had already noted in 1971 that Lewis Morris, writing to his brother Richard in 1760, had told him that the dish they called *llymru* in Anglesey was called *sucan* or *uwd* in Radnorshire; there are numerous other references to food in their letters, including the occasions on which they were eaten.

Earlier still, the work of the learned antiquarian George Owen (1552–1613) throws considerable light on social conditions in his native county of Pembrokeshire. Apparently modelling his *Description of Pembrokeshire* on the newly published *Survey of Cornwall* by Richard Carew which appeared in 1602, Owen belonged (as did Carew) to the school of chorographical authors of the late Elizabethan age, represented by William Lambarde and Sampson Erdeswicke who wrote comprehensively about the counties of Kent and Stafford respectively. Owen notes that the 'poorest husbandman liveth upon his owne travaille, having corne, butter, cheese, mutton, poultrie, and the like of his own sufficient to maintaine his house'. In the English-speaking part of south Pembrokeshire, 'theire dyett is as the English people use, as the common foode is Beefe, mutton, pigge, goose, lambe, veale and kydd which usuallye the poorest husbandman doth daylye feede on'. Owen, in accordance with his ideas on their ethnic origins, ascribes to their Flemish antecedents their excessive appetites: 'for of custom at certaine seasons and labors they will have fyve meals a daye, and if you will bestowe the sixt on them they will accept of it verye kindly, and they be but a little entreated, they will bestowe laboure on the seaventh meal.' How far regional differences in various parts of Wales had developed in response to local farming traditions and ecological conditions by Owen's day it is difficult to say, but it is clear that, in the eyes of a contemporary observer, the inhabitants of mid-seventeenth century Anglesey, for example, enjoyed a lower standard of food than their south Pembrokeshire counterparts. 'The tenants', he stated, '(are) very poore, living cheifly as most of the tenantes of these partes do, upon oate and barley bread and butter milk, and wheys, glasdwr [i.e. water and milk] and such like trash.'

Earlier evidence, particularly that of the medieval poets, relates mainly to the food served on the tables of the gentry who were open to cosmopolitan influences entering the country through the small market towns and ports. To cite one or two examples: Lewys Glyn Cothi (*fl.*1477–86) in a poem to Tomas ap Phylib of Picton Castle, Pembrokeshire, mentions specifically the wines of Bayonne, Mantes, Normandy, Bordeaux, Rochelle, Speyer, Spain and Brittany. The same poet in another *cywydd* tells us that his Radnorshire patron, Dafydd ap Rhys ap Meirig, would always have fish, birds in bread, pasties and good old drink – there would be enough to fill eight tables of sweet food, herbs from the shops for supper, a sewer of all kinds of herbs, dishes served in courses, white sugar, mead to intoxicate him, and other delicacies. Gastronomy was indeed a cultivated art in the houses of the Welsh gentry of the period and surviving manuscripts indicate that the niceties of service at the dinner table were regarded as an important part of their lifestyle. How the peasants fared we can only guess from the testimony of a later period, and it is from their tradition, not that of the gentry, that the various foods described by Minwel Tibbott derive. Hospitality and liberality, however, as she points out in her article on the subject in this volume, were not confined to the upper classes and were noted by the twelfth-century writer Giraldus Cambrensis whom she quotes at the beginning of her article.

Although initially concerned with the traditional scene, Minwel Tibbott also set out to record changes which had taken place in the kitchen, notably those which followed the introduction of new methods of cooking: changes occurring in our own day, she would have argued, are just as important to the ethnologist as old established methods which are disappearing and which, for that reason, have been given priority. Since the number of potential informants about recent innovations was very much greater, she decided to adopt a different approach when she was investigating the effects of the introduction of electricity into the kitchen. Her appeal in the press for information attracted a limited response in terms of numbers, but nevertheless enabled her to draw some interesting conclusions. Although the benefits of the new fuel to the housewife were obvious, cooking took second place to lighting and vacuum cleaning when electricity was installed. The oil cooking-stove, introduced between the two world wars seems to have made a greater impact, especially in the rural areas, enabling a steady controlled heat to be obtained, an advantage which the electric stove of the 1950s later possessed. A revolution occurred in what the ordinary housewife could effortlessly achieve, and sponge cakes took their place on the tea table alongside the traditional fruit breads and griddle cakes.

The electrical revolution in the form of the washing machine and vacuum cleaner also put paid to some of the traditional chores of housekeeping. Minwel Tibbott's article on laundering is the first detailed account of this neglected aspect of domestic life. The disappearance of the washerwoman – an occupation which was often the last resort of the penniless widow – marked a stage in the emancipation of the women of Wales, and the documentation of the endless tasks and the impedimenta involved reminds us that even the seemingly routine work of the housewife involved traditional skills in dealing with various materials. The housewife's pride in her home and in keeping it clean and tidy was reflected in the unusual practice of protecting table legs with old stockings, which was common in certain areas. Minwel Tibbott's research on this topic arose out of her recording of living conditions in the nineteenth-century houses removed from Rhyd-y-car, Merthyr Tydfil, to the Museum. Again she employed the technique of appealing to newspaper readers for information on the subject, in order to add to the material she had recorded from the lips of the inhabitants of Rhyd-y-car.

Modernization did not affect the other domestic skill discussed by Minwel Tibbott, namely knitting stockings. The knitting machine, apparently an invention of the twentieth century, never became popular: knitting was not a necessary domestic skill like cooking and laundering. It was the basis of a flourishing cottage industry among small farmers and cottagers in the sheep-rearing upland areas where wool was readily available, often as a result of either begging or wool-gathering. Knitting, however, was not restricted to the womenfolk: infirm or aged men, in particular, as well as menservants and children, could contribute to the household economy in this way. And the *noson wau* or knitting assembly which, as Minwel Tibbott points out, was an important social institution in upland Wales until the end of the nineteenth century, brought together neighbours of both sexes on moonlit winter evenings to combine work and leisure. Nevertheless, the trade which it created was largely in the hands of the women. It was they who took their stockings to the market or sold them to the hosiers, and it was their major contribution to the income of the home in the moorland districts.

This volume brings together the work of a dedicated scholar in a field which she had made her own, namely the contribution of womenfolk to the running of the traditional home in Wales. It is hoped, as she would have wished, that through her meticulous account of the domestic skills of cooking and housekeeping the reader will achieve a fuller understanding of the role of women in the past in Wales.

Trefor M. Owen

A Bibliography of S. Minwel Tibbott

1969	*Castell yr Iechyd – Elis Gruffydd*, University of Wales Press, Cardiff, 216pp.
1971	'Olrhain hanes bwydydd yng Nghymru', *Barn* (February), pp.126–8.
1973	'Traditional foods in Wales at the beginning of the twentieth century', *Ethnological Food Research*, Helsinki, p. 266–76.
1974	'*Sucan* and *llymru* in Wales', *Folk Life*, vol. 12, pp.31–40.
1974	*Amser Bwyd*, National Museum of Wales (Welsh Folk Museum), 84pp. Reprinted 1978.
1975	'Coginio traddodiadol: Traditional cooking', *Amgueddfa*, vol. 20, pp.13–27.
1976	*Welsh Fare*, National Museum of Wales (Welsh Folk Museum), 84pp.
1977	*Bwydydd Gwerin Cymru* (lecture published on cassette), National Museum of Wales (Welsh Folk Museum).
1978	'Knitting stockings in Wales – a domestic craft', *Folk Life*, vol. 16, pp.61–73.
1981	'Laundering in the Welsh home', *Folk Life*, vol. 19, pp.36–57.
1982	'Coginio traddodiadol: bara ceirch a rhai bwydydd eraill' (offprint from *Amgueddfa*, vol. 20, 1975).
1982	*Cooking on the Open Hearth*, National Museum of Wales (Welsh Folk Museum), 42pp.
1983	*Geirfa'r Gegin*, National Museum of Wales (Welsh Folk Museum), 212pp.
1983	'Y grefft o wau sanau yn ucheldir Cymru', *Journal of the Merioneth Historical and Record Society*, vol. 9, no. 3, pp.36–57.
1985–6	'Liberality and hospitality: food as communication in Wales', *Folk Life*, vol. 24, pp.32–51.
1986	'Food for free', *Transactions of the First International Food Congress*, ed. Feyzi Halici, pp.293–302.

1988   'Furnishing, fashions and fetish: a Welsh study', *The Local Historian*, vol. 18, no. 4, pp.168–73.*

1988   'Bara ceirch – y bwyd a'r grefft', *Melin* vol. 4, pp.38–57.

1989–90 'Going electric: the changing face of the rural kitchen in Wales, 1945–55', *Folk Life*, vol. 28, pp.63–73.

1991   *Baking in Wales*, National Museum of Wales, 36pp.**

1991   *The Gwalia: The Story of a Valleys Shop* (with Beth Thomas), National Museum of Wales, 43pp.

1994   *O'r Gwaith i'r Gwely: Cadw Tŷ 1890–1960 / A Woman's Work: Housework 1890–1960* (with Beth Thomas), National Museum of Wales, 43pp.

1995–6 'Cheese-making in Glamorgan', *Folk Life*, vol. 34, pp.64–79.

*   Published here as 'Modesty, protection or display? The covering of table legs in Wales', pp.129–39.

** 'Traditional breads of Wales' (pp.78–112) is a revised version of this publication.

List of Plates

Liberality and Hospitality:
Food as Communication in Wales

No one of this nation ever begs; for the houses of all are common to all; and they consider liberality and hospitality amongst the first virtues. So much does hospitality here rejoice in communication, that it is neither offered nor requested by travellers, who, on entering any house, only deliver up their arms. When water is offered to them, if they suffer their feet to be washed, they are received as guests.

Gerallt Gymro (Giraldus Cambrensis), *The Description of Wales*[1]

Eating may be regarded not only as a physiological function in maintaining life, but also as an experience that plays a significant role in establishing relationships between members of society. Day by day a meal is an opportunity for family and work-team to communicate. Through the centuries, members of a particular household have been brought together to one convenient point to share the experience of eating in order to sustain life. However, oral testimony reveals discrimination between family and work-team during mealtimes was evident in many of the larger farms throughout Wales at the turn of the century. It was discerned not only in the content of the meals themselves, but also in the seating arrangements.

In the counties of south and west Wales many large farmhouses were equipped with a table room or board room (*rhwm ford*). It was sparsely furnished with a long table and two wooden benches to accommodate the servants and labourers during mealtimes, while the master and mistress ate in the best kitchen (*cegin orau*). In the other more modest farmhouses, two separate tables were located in the work kitchen. Here the master and mistress would sit at a round table near the fire, while the servants sat around the long table near the window. The children joined the servants in the board room or at the long table, as soon as they were capable of eating without supervision. Visiting labourers and craftsmen, present at mealtimes, were also offered meals in the board room, while the visiting seamstress was always invited to share a table with the master and mistress and was offered the best fare of the house.

Of the hired servants on a farm, the chief servant (*gwas mawr*) was known by that title, the others as a second servant, third servant and so on, according to the number employed. During mealtimes the chief servant would be the first to be served, if waited upon by the maid, and he would supervise the time allocated for the meal, which was usually limited to some twenty minutes. In the period when the men used their own clasp-knives at the table, everyone was expected to finish eating and leave the table when the chief servant closed his knife.[2] An echo of this custom is heard in the familiar phrase used casually at the table in this rural community even today. When induced to eat, people are urged 'Bytwch, mae pob gair yn damaid' ('Eat up, every word is a bite').

A similar seating arrangement was found in the counties of north Wales. In the hinterland of Denbighshire, Merioneth and Montgomeryshire two tables were placed in the work kitchen, with the master and mistress taking position at the small table near the fire. The chief male servant (*hwsmon*) would supervise every meal on the long table, and he would be responsible for slicing the bread for the other servants. He would be the first to stand up at the end of a meal and the others would walk out in front of him, each man to his task.[3] In the larger farms in the coastal regions of the Llŷn peninsula and in Anglesey, two separate rooms were provided, with the family eating in the best kitchen or hall (*neuadd*) and the menservants in the work kitchen or *briws* (brewhouse). The position of the maid in respective regions was not hard and fast; in some households she would join the family at the table, in others she would be relegated to the servants' room.

Informants who had been employed in service on farms in different parts of the country were not too informative regarding the quality and quantity of food offered to them, but they readily spoke of the different types of bread served at the two tables. In all areas it was common practice to give barley bread or an inferior 'mixed' bread to the servants for every meal on a weekday, while the family ate white bread. As a special treat the servants would be offered one slice of white bread for their Sunday tea. Pottage would be served regularly to the servants for breakfast while the family enjoyed tea with bread and butter. On the Llŷn peninsula, even in the early decades of the twentieth century, the pottage known as *brwes* (brose) was served to the menservants in one large communal bowl. Four or six men would take position around it, every man keeping to his pre-marked portion. On many farms, breakfast was followed by household devotions, which comprised a short reading from the Bible and a prayer. In the two-room situation, the master would join the servants in the board room, where he or a mature servant conducted the service.[4] In this context, elderly informants often quoted a four-line stanza which was supposedly included in a prayer offered by a colleague during this household devotion. Referring to the quality of the food served to them at a particular farm, they would call on God to bless the poor fare offered to them, or pray for the better-quality food known to be reserved in the dairy:

Arglwydd grasol dyma fwyd
Cawl sur a bara llwyd,
Dyro fendith ar y cawlach
Mae pob peth yn eitha' afiach

Caws a menyn yn y dairy
Arglwydd annwyl, danfon rheiny

[Gracious God, what food
Sour pottage and mouldy bread,
Give your blessing on the mess
Everything is quite unhealthy

Butter and cheese is in the dairy
Dear God, please send us these]

Without doubt, this frugal diet was the inevitable result of the agricultural depressions experienced in Wales during the nineteenth century. Hence, as an attempt to overcome the food shortage, meals, even at the turn of the twentieth century, continued to be a divisive factor in the master–servant situation.

HOSPITALITY

Despite the shortage of provisions in most households, however, hospitality prevailed as a prominent characteristic of the Welsh people. Thomas Pennant wrote of the welcome he was given by one Evan Lloyd of Cwm Bychan near Harlech in the heart of Merioneth in the eighteenth century:

> I was introduced to the worthy representative of this long line who gave me the most hospitable reception and in style of an ancient Briton. He welcomed us with ale and potent beer to wash down *coch yr wden*, or hung goat, and the cheese compounded of the milk of cow and sheep.[5]

The fare offered to guests by this landed gentleman was simple, but the height of hospitality was expressed in the invitation to partake of a meal. It is a tradition that a casual visitor, whether he be a friend or stranger, is invited into a Welsh home and is rarely allowed to leave without joining the family at the table. George Borrow described the welcome he received while visiting the home of a miller and his wife in Anglesey in the mid-nineteenth century. Having called on them unexpectedly, he was invited to the table which had already been laid for a meal of bread and butter and 'a few very thin slices of brown, watery cheese'. The wife poured out tea for the stranger, but before he could taste it she produced a basin full of snow-white lump sugar and 'placed two of the largest lumps in my cup, though she helped neither her husband or herself; the sugar basin being probably only kept for grand occasions'.[6]

A shortage of provisions at the beginning of the twentieth century did not blunt the welcome extended to a visitor. Indeed, food was the symbol of welcome, and the hospitality would demonstrate a special respect or affection towards the guest, and indicate a certain sacrifice by the hostess. The most general luxury item offered for afternoon tea throughout the country would be pancakes or drop-scones. The hostess would proceed to bake them after the arrival of an unexpected guest, and they would be served warm, spread liberally with butter and home-made jam. A boiled egg was regarded as a treat in many households when the bulk of the eggs were sold and not consumed by the family. White sugar, a tin of salmon and yeasted buns (wigs) were also noted as luxury items bought especially for the unexpected guest. Purchasing these items would require a monetary sacrifice by the hostess.

CELEBRATIONS AND FEASTS

Personal celebrations, family gatherings and annual festivals offer regular opportunities for social intercourse wherein food forms a focal point. In rural Wales, a funeral, for example, to this day is attended by a large gathering of relatives, friends and neighbours to pay their last respects to the deceased. The bereaved family has always considered it a duty and a privilege to provide the funeral attenders with some refreshment. In Anglesey, in the eighteenth century, they would be given 'a cup of drink, & if deceased be rich servd with cakes, wine &c'.[7] In Llanfechain, Montgomeryshire, one of the church communion vessels was used to distribute spiced ale at funerals until the middle of the nineteenth century.[8] According to another writer, an elaborate meal was eaten before the funeral and three or even four hours spent smoking shag-tobacco, and drinking ale in the house before forming the cortège. Sometimes wine and finger biscuits were handed round after the guests had formed the funeral procession.[9] In another district in the same county the currant cakes, eaten before the funeral procession left, are described as being 'about two inches square, with a kind of biscuit about three inches long by one inch broad across each'. These were handed out on trays just as the body was brought out of the house and placed on the bier.[10] Hot spiced ale and cake seem to have been offered on this occasion in many areas in south Wales also, until the second half of the nineteenth century. From this time onwards the pattern so developed that the funeral attenders returned from the burial to the house of the deceased for a meal of bread and butter, tea, home-boiled ham, pickled onions and fruit cake. A chapel vestry or a schoolroom would be used as alternative venues. Even today a similar meal is prepared for the immediate family and friends, especially in rural areas. It provides an opportunity for all members to exchange family news and discuss other topics of mutual interest.

Annual festivals such as Christmas and New Year can also be regarded as social functions when members of a community congregate in order to celebrate. At all times, the celebrating has always been closely linked with food. Christmas in Wales in the first half of the nineteenth century was celebrated by attending an early-morning *plygain* service in the local church.[11] Preceding this service, young folk would congregate in one of the homes to attend an informal toffee-making party. After the *plygain* service friends and relatives would visit each other, and be offered traditional fare of hot ale, cakes and cold meats while the goose was cooking for dinner. Nowadays the *plygain* service is usually held in the evening, and is often followed by a supper. By the late nineteenth and early twentieth centuries, Christmas developed to be more of a family celebration, and the festivities provided them with an occasion to enjoy better quality fare than they could afford during the remainder of the year. During this season of goodwill it was tradition to share this fare with friends and neighbours. In most districts throughout the country, oral testimony proves that the majority of families would celebrate Christmas with a roast goose or a joint of beef for dinner at midday, followed by rice or plum pudding. Christmas tea would be marked with a rich yeasted fruit cake.

Plygain supper served to carollers by the Watkins family at Cefn Llwyd farm near Llanfair Caereinion, 23 December 1973. (By courtesy of J. Tegwyn Roberts)

In some rural areas of south Wales and more especially Cardiganshire and Carmarthenshire, it was the practice among farmers to invite harvest-time helpers to join them at the farm for Christmas dinner. Complete families would be invited, and to have a party of some twenty-five members on the larger farms was not unusual. Goose, plum pudding, home-brewed beer, games and merriment would be enjoyed by both young and old throughout the day. In Pembrokeshire this custom was practised on New Year's Day or on Old New Year's Day (that is, 13 January). Christmas Day was not celebrated in this part of the country until fairly recently.[12]

Toffee-pulling at Tŷ Du, Parc near Bala, 1971.

Similar traditional fare was enjoyed by families in both the agricultural and industrial areas of north Wales at the beginning of the twentieth century. Here, families would invite neighbours and friends to each other's homes on Christmas Eve, or on a specific evening during the festive season to attend an informal toffee-making party. Following a traditional supper of goose and plum pudding, the celebrating continued with merriment focused around the toffee-making. When the required ingredients had boiled to a certain degree, the toffee was poured on to a well-greased slate or stone slab. The hearth stone itself was used for this purpose in some houses. Members of the happy gathering would then smear their hands with butter and attempt to 'pull' the toffee while it was warm. It was a skilled art to 'pull' and twist the toffee until it became golden brown in colour. Both the skilled and the unskilled alike would take part, the one being a source of envy, the other a source of banter.

Before the introduction of sophisticated machinery, every farmer was dependent on the cooperation of his neighbours to accomplish seasonal work. According to the nature of the farm, major tasks such as hay or corn harvesting, corn threshing or sheep shearing were essentially communal efforts, governed by certain established unwritten rules. In some instances a dozen farms would join forces to form a work-team to fulfil the task in hand.

Hay harvesting was of paramount importance to every farmer, and his work-team would be rewarded with special fare. One author writing of this harvest in south-west Wales early in the twentieth century notes: 'hay-making was the happiest and gayest of all seasonal activities by reason of the big, merry and animate company that came together'.[13] The usual number was twenty-five to thirty people, male and female, including boys and girls who were able to assist with the lighter tasks. In south Wales, both the midday meal and afternoon snack would be served out in the field, usually in a shady spot. This arrangement accelerated the work, as valuable time was saved by not having to walk a fair distance back to the house. The womenfolk would carry the food to the field in large baskets and lay it out on the ground. The traditional

Hay harvest helpers enjoying a rather sumptuous meal, at Brynna, Llanharan, Glamorgan, c.1910.

dish served for this midday meal on the hayfield was a cold sour-grain soup known as *uwd* or *sucan*. Boiled to the required consistency, it was poured into large tin pans to cool. Before carrying it out to the field, particular attention would be paid to the surface of the dish after it had set. Tradition had it that a smooth, even surface, free from cracks and with a slight sheen on it was a maiden-cook's pride and joy. It proved her skill in boiling the mixture to the desired consistency. A cracked surface, on the other hand, indicated that the maiden-cook was destined to marry an ugly fellow, and to present such a dish on the hayfield would subject her to great mockery. The workers would help themselves to this oat-jelly, and put it in cold milk or beer. Most elderly informants recalled that this dish would be supplemented with a second course of bread and butter or roast potatoes. However, after the First World War, this light meal was superseded by a more sumptuous meal consisting of a meat-based pottage and a rice pudding. Afternoon tea would consist of tea, home-baked bread, butter and jam and another harvest-time speciality – yeasted currant loaf. Home-brewed beer, a lighter harvest ginger-beer, or water laced with oatmeal would be brought around to the workers periodically during the course of the day. At the end of the day the work-team would be invited into the house for a supper of home-cured ham, reserved for the harvest season, new potatoes and other home-grown vegetables, followed by rice pudding or apple dumplings.

Traditional fare most closely associated with the hay harvest in the hinterland counties of north Wales was a dish known as *siot*. It consisted simply of crushed oatcake steeped in cold buttermilk. Such was the demand for this thirst-quenching and satisfying dish by the workers in the field that ladies skilled in the craft of making oatcakes would be employed on large farms to bake a sufficient supply to tide them over the harvest period. *Siot* was a suitable dish for carrying out to the fields in large cans, and it would be served usually as an afternoon refreshment. In these regions, all other meals would be served in the house.

Mealtimes and short intervals for refreshment on the field gave workers a welcome opportunity for bantering and joviality. Young women, clad in their well-laundered blouses and white knee-length pinafores, were a great attraction to the opposite sex. Hay-harvest games where the men chased the girls around the haycocks, and young men vying with each other in feats of strength, are among the recollections quoted by informants.

Oats and barley were grown to some extent on most farms throughout the country. However, the corn harvest would be celebrated as a major event within the wheat belts of the fertile valleys and coastal regions. In these areas, reaping teams (*medelwyr*) of some fifteen to twenty men would circulate among a specific number of neighbouring farms to cut the wheat, formerly with sickles but latterly with scythes. A lady would follow each man to bind the sheaves. In parts of Glamorgan and Carmarthenshire, a special wheat-reaper's dish called *whipod* (whitepot) was prepared for this annual event. Consisting of rice, milk, currants, raisins, eggs, spice and flour, first the mixture would be boiled and then transferred into large tins for slow baking in the brick-oven. The reapers and their families were invited for an evening meal of roast meat, usually lamb, and vegetables, followed by the whitepot as a second-course delicacy. After partaking of this feast as reward for their labour during the day, all members of the party would join together for a social evening of dancing and games.

In other districts of west Wales, the reapers' supper would be celebrated in conjunction with the *caseg fedi* (harvest mare). The *caseg fedi* was an ornament made from the final tuft of corn that had been left uncut in the corner of the last field. It was plaited by the reapers who then stood away at a distance of some twenty yards to throw their sickles at it, in turn. The reaper who was successful in cutting it through would rush away with it, concealed on his person, to the farmhouse. The aim was to carry it dry into the house, escaping the attention of a servant girl who would be waiting outside the door, armed with a bucket of water. Following this great feat, a feast of *poten ben fedi* (harvest pie) would be served. This same celebration was known as *ffest y pen* (end of harvest feast) or *ffest y wrach* (the hag's feast). At the end of the nineteenth century this harvest pie usually consisted of mashed potatoes mixed with minced beef, bacon and onion. At a later date the pie was superseded by a cold beef supper.

Another festive occasion associated with the harvest, but usually postponed until November, was celebrated in specific parts of west Wales. Harvest workers and their families were invited to a harvest dinner by a particular farmer, and in some instances this celebration would coincide with the slaughtering of a beast. This provided the farmer with a plentiful supply of fresh meat. It must be realized that the ordinary fare of the period would be restricted to salt-meat dishes. To be invited to partake of a sumptuous meal of fresh roast meat was a welcome treat for the cottagers and other landless families. The purpose of the festivity would be the renewing of ties of friendship within the community, as well as showing gratitude for cooperating during the harvest season. It also ensured help would again be forthcoming in the following season.

A typical social gathering at a farmhouse on sheep-shearing day, with the female members waiting on the menfolk during the mid-day meal, Plas Tan-y-bont, Cwm Cywarch, 1984. (By courtesy of Niall MacLeod)

Cooperative activity was extended to corn threshing which took place when the pressure of work on the farm had eased. This was another occasion for social intercourse among farming families – the cooperation in fulfilling the task and in preparing food for the work-team involved a large number of people. So similarly, in the moorland regions where the emphasis was on sheep farming, shearing day demanded the same cooperation, with every farm within a group being allocated a specific day for this annual event. It would bring together neighbours, relatives and friends from a large area. Poor transport facilities hampered frequent communication during the year, so this event was also regarded as a welcome opportunity to exchange items of family news, as well as to discuss other topics of regional interest. The female members were involved in preparing elaborate meals for these important social events. The best china and cutlery were brought out, and every effort was made to give the guests a worthy welcome. A lady who had been in service in a large moorland farm in mid-Wales recalled the marathon task of catering for a hundred people over two whole days while shearing some seven thousand sheep. It took a whole week to prepare food for this occasion; the work-team and guests would be served with a dinner of cold roast beef, potatoes and peas, followed with a creamy rice pudding; afternoon tea would be a plain meal of home-baked bread, butter, cheese and jam. A rich yeasted fruit cake or a gooseberry pie were both regarded as shearing specialities in some regions. Similar fare would be served to the threshing parties in the lowland areas. In both instances, a family's prestige was linked with the lavishness of a well-prepared feast.

FOOD AS GIFTS

In Wales, food has been employed as a symbol to express happiness, sympathy or appreciation within a close community. Major events punctuating the day-to-day lifestyle of a particular family, in turn, would generate goodwill among friends and neighbours, and gifts of food would be offered to express their sentiments as opportunities arose. Despite the fact that rural households strove to be self-sufficient at all times, luxury items of food were more acceptable to them than monetary gifts. In remote areas, access to shops was difficult, and consequently monetary gifts were deemed less valuable.

In both rural and industrial areas, if a mother or wife was incapacitated due to illness or childbirth, gifts of food were very welcome to help the family through the crisis period. After the birth of a child, it was customary for female friends to visit the mother within a few days after the event. They would not go empty-handed, but usually took with them gifts of bread, butter, tea or sugar. In the coal-mining valleys home-made cakes were also regarded as a special gift. This custom of visiting after childbirth was known as *mynd i weld* (lit. going to see) *cyflwyno* or *cyflwyna* (to offer)[14] or *mynd i wledda* (to go feasting).[15] Of course, the visitor was not allowed to return home without partaking of a light meal with the family, and in some instances the local 'midwife' temporarily 'employed' by the family would be expected to lay the table and prepare this meal. The mother would welcome the pleasant hour spent discussing the special attributes of the newly born, and exchanging views on local news or events.

Visiting a sick friend was another custom which qualified for gifts of food. In this instance the item of food taken to the invalid would have special medicinal attributes to speed recovery. Informants in some rural districts of north Wales referred to the local custom of taking a bowlful of *llymru* (sour-grain jelly) as a delicacy to whet the appetite. Other nourishing gifts offered to the sick were milk, butter, eggs and home-made preserves. In the quarrying districts of north Wales, however, the luxury item mostly associated with sick-visiting was a currant bun. Informants recalled the custom of buying buns at the local bakery; known as 'wigs', these buns were of a lighter texture than ordinary white bread and were also slightly sweeter. Split open, toasted and generously spread with fresh farm butter they were particularly appetizing to the invalid.

On the occasion of a wedding and the establishing of a young couple in their new home, items of food were specifically listed as suggested gifts. In south-west Wales in the eighteenth and nineteenth centuries, the marriage celebrations included a festivity to which people were invited or bidden by word of mouth. A person known as the *gwahoddwr* (bidder) was appointed by the bride or groom's family to announce the forthcoming marriage. It was his duty to visit the homes of relatives, neighbours and friends to deliver the formal invitation. Having announced the date and venue of the marriage ceremony and the wedding feast (*neithior*), he would proceed to recite a list of suggested gifts to be rendered at the feast. A bidder's invitation, as recorded in the first half of the nineteenth century, reads 'or send a waggon full of potatoes, a cartload of turnips, a hundred or two of cheeses, a cask of butter, a sack of flour, a winchester of barley, or what you please, for anything will be acceptable'.[16] Wedding lists therefore are not modern innovations. Today, items of food are no longer regarded as suitable wedding gifts, with the one exception of the bride occasionally being presented with a rich and elaborately decorated wedding cake.

Sympathy towards a bereaved family on experiencing a death in the house would also be expressed with gifts of food. Extra provisions would help support the family during the immediate period of grief, or be a contribution towards the funeral tea. During the nineteenth century, expensive items such as tea and sugar would be given by friends and neighbours who called to sympathize with the family. This custom still prevails in rural Wales today. Gifts of tea, sugar and home-baked cakes are sympathy symbols which are specifically contributed towards the funeral tea.

One more custom which was prevalent in the rural areas of south and west Wales during the agricultural depression of the nineteenth century was to give gifts of food to well-wishers on New Year's Day. This ancient custom was known as *hela Calennig* and was observed widely in the southern half of the country. The collection of gifts began early in the day and continued until noon. An account published in 1819 described the custom as practised by the children only: 'New Year is marked by all children in the neighbourhood, forming themselves in little groups and carrying from house to house their congratulations and good wishes for health and prosperity during the ensuing year . . .'[17] Verses were sung at the door of the house, and a small gift given to the members of the party in response. Sometimes the verse would incorporate a specific request for food:

> Mi godais heddiw ma's o'm tŷ
> A'm cwd a'm pastwn gyda mi
> A dyma'm neges ar eich traws
> Sef llanw'm cwd â bara a chaws[18]

> [I came today out of my house
> With a bag and a stick
> My errand here is to fill
> My bag with bread and cheese]

Another author writing of this custom in Pembrokeshire in the nineteenth century reports that people would walk distances of twenty or thirty miles, gathering white loaves at different houses. Young women and girls, dressed in their best clothes, were grateful recipients of this luxury item, which was a welcome change from their daily diet of barley bread.[19] Informants from this part of the country recalled that the custom was still in practice at the turn of the century, with both children and women being offered gifts of bread and cheese at the larger farmhouses. To meet this demand, farmhouse-wives would allocate a special baking session to cater for the well-wishers. Yeasted buns known as *pice* or *cace* were also provided by some households.

This custom of collecting gifts of food on New Year's Day has not been recorded in north Wales. However, gifts of oatmeal were readily given to poor women during the early winter months. When the farmers had replenished their oatmeal chests after a good harvest, it was general custom to give a bowlful of oatmeal to the occasional visitor who called to *hel cardod* (to collect charity). Yet, the recipients who came from landless families were never made to feel that they were subjects of charity; gifts were given in a kindly manner, promoting good neighbourly spirit within the community.

PAYMENT IN KIND

Food used as payment in kind can be traced back to the early medieval period in Welsh history. The Laws of Hywel Dda (Hywel the Good), codified in the tenth century, stipulate that wheatbread or oatbread could be given as part of the food-tithe payable to the king by both bondmen and freemen alike.[20]

Food as payment for services rendered has also been an accepted arrangement in rural areas. Up until the end of the nineteenth century, the *gwahoddwr* (bidder) employed to announce a wedding, or the *rhybuddiwr* (announcer) similarly engaged to announce a funeral, were both recipients of food items as acknowledgement of their service. A bidder, employed in Laugharne in the 1840s, was described thus: 'he would be dressed in a white apron, a white ribbon was tied in the buttonhole of his coat and the bidder's staff in his hand with which he knocked at doors . . . a bag swung at his back, in which he put the bread and cheese the people at the farmhouses gave the bidder'.[21] Oatmeal was also regarded as a useful provision which would be invaluable to their families for making pottage or oatcakes throughout the winter months. Bread, butter, milk or potatoes were other acceptable commodities given to the local midwife or washerwoman as payment for their services on farms.

In most rural areas up until the early years of the twentieth century, harvest-time help was acknowledged with gifts of food. At this period, wives of tenants and cottagers would help with the hay-harvest on the larger farms. For their service, the farmers would give them a regular supply of buttermilk during the whole year, in addition to a specific measure of oatmeal, known in Cardiganshire as *blawd swper adre* (home supper meal) One measureful per day of work was the usual payment. A loaf of bread would be an alternative payment, but in either case a wedge of cheese would also be given. Gifts of bread and cheese as payment for harvest-time labour, in some instances, were delivered to the helpers on New Year's Day. One informant recalled how the menservants of particular farms would deliver wheaten loaves and wedges of cheese to the helpers' homes by horse and cart. Allocation of space for planting potatoes on the farmers' land was also a reward for harvest-time help. Tenants, cottagers and miners took advantage of this arrangement with one day's work-debt being equal to one row of potatoes.

In most districts a reciprocal arrangement involving neighbouring farmers, tenants and cottagers was the custom of exchanging fresh meat joints when slaughtering a pig. Slaughtering would be carried out systematically within a community, usually between early October and late March, thus supplying families with a joint of fresh meat at regular intervals throughout this period. Pork steaks and joints incorporating the ribs and back chine were the usual cuts delivered. Dishes prepared from the pig's offal (such as faggots and brawn) were also bonus gifts exchanged between friends and relatives, and this custom was practised in parts of south Wales well into the second half of the twentieth century. The pleasant task of delivering the cuts of meat was generally allocated to the children, who invariably were recipients of a small monetary reward. In some districts, this custom was known as *hebrwng asgwrn* (sending a bone). The remainder of the pig would be salted, and would serve as the staple-meat supply to the respective households through-out the year.

Pig-killing day at Maescar, Brecknockshire, c.1900. All members of the family helped the butcher to debristle the pig.

FOOD AS SOCIAL AID

Traditional foods were evident as means of providing social aid in all types of communities during the nineteenth and early twentieth centuries. In the industrial towns and villages of both north and south Wales, selling traditional dishes from the home or on the local market stall was a prominent cottage industry. In the absence of social monetary benefits during periods of sickness, industrial strife or death of the breadwinner, the income gained from selling home-prepared items of food or drink was of great aid to the vendor and her family. On the other hand, the service provided by them was of equal value to the local community, and the contact made between parties during the transaction of buying, selling and consuming generated friendship and social activity.

In the coal-mining villages of south Wales, one of the favourite dishes prepared for selling was faggots. An observer, visiting Merthyr Tydfil market in 1881, witnessed the selling of home-made faggots there:

> A pile of what I took to be sausages were steaming furiously over a brazier of burning coals on one end of the bench, with a teapot leaning lazily against it and thinking aloud. Choosing what seemed the least formidable specimen of the food before me, I pointed to the brazier, but in a tone so low I was not heard 'I will take a sausage'. Obeying my gesture, the woman served me a saucer-full of the black balls, swimming in hot gravy, and gave me a pewter spoon with which to eat it, instead of the knife and fork which might have been expected with meat. The balls proved to be not unpalatable eating, and were, according to my best judgement, made of liver.[22]

These forcemeat balls were prepared from pig's liver, lights, small pieces of pork fat and the thin membrane known as caul. The liver, lights and pork pieces were chopped finely, to which were added chopped onions, breadcrumbs, a little sage and seasoning. All were well mixed together. The caul was then cut into six-inch squares, each piece being wrapped around a tablespoonful of the mixture to form a faggot. Placed side by side in large roasting tins, they were cooked in a moderately hot oven. They would be served cold with bread and butter for lunch or a supper snack, but it was also a tradition to serve them hot with peas and gravy. Miners' wives or widows striving to augment the family income would buy pig's liver and lights regularly from the local butcher for a nominal sum of money. They would prepare this delicacy with peas to sell from their own homes.

Faggots for sale on a market stall at Carmarthen, 1980.

Informants from the mining villages of south-east Wales related how their grandmothers, at the turn of the century, prepared and cooked faggots on specific days of the week throughout the year. Regular customers from the neighbourhood would bring along an earthen jug or bowl to carry home the required number of faggots in gravy and another bowl for peas. First-hand information of this 'cottage' industry was given by one lady informant who had practised it herself as late as 1953. Selling some hundred faggots at two pence each every Friday evening provided her with a sum of money to buy a joint of fresh meat for her own family's Sunday lunch. Home-made faggots are still sold today by some well-established stall-holders in the market towns of south Wales – ample proof of their profitability.

A comparable savoury dish prepared for marketing in north Wales was pickled herrings. Herring fishing was a major industry common to all coastal villages and towns in Wales, but the selling of this traditional dish was confined to the coastal towns and slate-quarrying villages of the northern counties. Placed in an earthenware dish with onion rings, pickling spices and vinegar, water and seasoning, the herrings were baked very slowly until the bones disintegrated. This dish was prepared on specific days by ladies anxious to augment their income, and customers would flock to their homes to buy the pickled herrings for two pence each. Menservants were known to congregate in a particular vendor's house and to while away their time in a convivial atmosphere on a Saturday evening consuming this delicacy. Others would buy them at midday and eat them in their own homes with jacket potatoes and oatcakes.

Other favourite items prepared in ordinary homes in the counties of south Wales for marketing were yeasted currant buns (*pice cwrens*) and bread pudding (*pwdin bara*), while in north Wales oatcakes and muffins were the stock items sold. The art of oatcake-making was prolonged in slate-quarrying districts by those ladies who practised it in order to augment their income. Similarly, in the agricultural areas, ladies proficient in the same craft were employed as casual labour on larger farms to bake a substantial supply of oatcakes for the harvest period or for the winter months.

Home-made toffee and small beer were luxury items common to the industrial towns and villages of both north and south Wales and which were sold by ordinary housewives. Home-made toffee, known as *cyflaith* or *india roc* in the north, or as *taffi dant*, or *losin dant* in the south, would be sold regularly from home or on local market stalls. One particular family in the coal-mining district, at the turn of the century, developed their toffee-making business to the extent that they eventually established a sweet-manufacturing business. Their shop, meeting the demands of the mining community, became a centre where people met, while purchasing the slab-toffee, to exchange views on cultural and religious topics.[23]

Diod fain or *diod ddail* (small beer) was a favourite drink with the coal-miner and slate-quarry worker alike: as a thirst quencher it was drunk daily by members of both communities. Local demand proved profitable to many widows or others anxious to find a source of income. They would brew it weekly in large quantities to sell to regular customers for two pence per quart bottle. One lady informant from Glamorgan related how she collected large quantities of nettle-leaf tips and dandelion leaves, in season. They were washed, dried and stored in clean sacks to provide her with a continuous supply throughout the whole year. A quantity of these leaves, together with ground ivy, redcurrant leaves and root ginger, was boiled; the liquid was then strained and sweetened with sugar. Yeast was added to the cooled mixture, which was allowed to stand overnight. On the following day it was poured and corked securely. In the early decades of the twentieth century, this one informant recalled selling an average of forty-two bottles per week making a profit of seven shillings, a sum which at that date was an invaluable addition to the low family income. She was representative of many other industrious ladies who supplied their own neighbourhood with this delectable drink.

Communities living close to the coast have also taken advantage of the source of food available to them on the beach or coastal rocks.[24] There is extensive evidence from prehistoric and Roman sites that shellfish were included in the diet of early man, and have been harvested in Wales throughout the centuries. Free for the collecting, shellfish have been found in profusion along the coast, the types most commonly collected and marketed by ordinary people being cockles and mussels. During the latter half of the nineteenth and the early decades of the twentieth century, female cockle-gatherers were regular stall-holders at urban markets in south Wales, while others sold their harvest from door to door in industrial and coastal villages in both north and south Wales. Cockles, boiled and removed from their shells (*cocs rhython*), were usually carried in a wooden pail, balanced on the vendor's head, while the untreated variety (*cocs cregyn*) were carried in a large basket on the arm. One informant from Llan-saint, a coastal village in south Wales, who had experienced some sixty years of beachcombing for cockles until she reached her eightieth year, referred to the usual pattern of daughters succeeding mothers in this occupation. They were dependent on this source of income. She recalled selling cockles for a halfpenny a pint, but toward the end of her career the same quantity was sold for sixpence, still a very mean reward for the tedious work involved. Gathering, washing and transporting them home from the beach was the initial stage, which had to be followed by a second process of washing, boiling and further transporting for marketing.

Cockles provided a light meal served with bread and butter or oatcakes, and were included in various dishes with eggs or with milk and chives. When selling the shellfish, the women in the village of Penrhyndeudraeth, Merioneth, would refer to the alternative method of serving them in the following rhyme, while singing and dancing their way from door to door:

> Cocos a wya
> Bara ceirch tena
> Merched y Penrhyn
> Yn ysgwyd 'u tina[25]

> [Eggs and cockles
> Thin oatcake
> The girls of Penrhyn
> Their bottoms ashake]

Another important food product from the sea was laver, an edible seaweed. In the eighteenth and nineteenth centuries, women living in the coastal regions of Anglesey, Glamorgan and Pembrokeshire were ardent gatherers of laver. According to informants experienced in this work, the laver collected from seashore rocks and stones had to be washed in seven changes of water to rid it of all its grit and sand. All excess moisture was then removed, and the clean laver boiled away slowly in its own moisture for some seven hours. Finally, it was drained and chopped very finely to give a greeny-black pulp. Tossed in oatmeal and fried in bacon fat, it was usually served with bacon. Know as *bara lawr*, *llafan* or *menyn y môr*, laverbread was prepared as a commercial product by Glamorgan families, and was sold along with the cockles on the market stalls. Formerly, these two items were prepared and sold strictly by low-income families. Eventually their marketing was developed into commercial enterprises of considerable importance. Today, laverbread, often given the alternative name of Welsh caviar, has found its way on to delicatessen counters and is offered as an hors d'œuvre in first-class restaurants.

FEASTS AND PARTIES

The motive to organize specific feasts and parties in the rural districts of Wales up until the later decades of the nineteenth century was twofold. People were invited to attend a social function to enjoy a celebration or festivity and to participate in the general social intercourse experienced within a close-knit community. But the key motive for promoting the function would be pecuniary gain. When inviting guests to attend a wedding in south-west Wales in the 1840s, a bidder's proclamation included the following details regarding the feast:

> They shall have good beef and cabbage, mutton and turnips, pork and potatoes, roast goose or gant, perhaps both if they are in season, *a quart of drink for 4d, a cake for a penny*, clean chairs to sit down upon.[26] [author's emphasis]

Selling cakes and ale was a prominent feature of a wedding feast during this period, and the sum of money gained in this way was given to the newly married couple to help them set up home. A special brew of beer would be prepared at the home of the bride and groom, and small cakes or buns known as *cacs* would be baked by the bride's friends. *Pobi neithior* (a bidding bake) would usually take place on the eve of the wedding. *Cacs neithior* (bidding cakes) have been described as being thin and tough quadrangles, some five inches long by three inches wide, and they were sold to make clear profit. During the feast they would be taken around by the bidder, and it was the usual custom for the young men to buy them for two pence each.[27] They would offer one as a gift to entice an attractive young girl from her suitor. To have received a large number of cakes during the evening would prove a young girl's popularity with the opposite sex, and to go home laden with a bagful of cakes was an achievement of which every girl was proud. Each transaction also proved profitable to the bride and groom.[28] On the Gower peninsula, *pastai neithior* (a bidding pie) would be stipulated as the purchasable item at a wedding feast. A local farmer would supply the meat by killing a sheep for the occasion, and the womenfolk would join forces to prepare and cook the pies. A small piece would be sold for a sum that would vary between five and ten shillings and would be served cold with beer, the actual sum of money paid by each guest would be recorded by the bidder, and the young beneficiaries, in turn, would be invited to similar feasts and would be expected to repay their 'debt' to the bride or groom's respective families.[29]

Wedding feasts in certain parts of north Wales were open to all well-wishers in the neighbourhood without formal invitation. They were welcome to partake of a dinner which consisted of wheatbread and sweet milk for a charge of one shilling.[30]

Ox-roasting at St Fagans, Glamorgan, *c.*1900.

Another official function, prominent in the counties of south-west Wales until the end of the nineteenth century, was known as *cwrw bach* (lit. 'small beer'). This party would be held solely to help low-income families who were victims of a major crisis or loss which would impair their livelihood. Ill health of a husband or wife, or the loss of a horse or a cow on the farm, would bring friends and neighbours together to organize a money-raising party, which was usually held at the victim's home. To realize a worthy sum of money, the organizers would brew a large supply of good-quality beer. Men and women from the surrounding districts would attend the party without formal invitation, partaking of the beer and light refreshments of bread and cheese for a small charge. Eventually at these parties beer was replaced by tea, but the function was still held under the original title of *cwrw bach*. This social activity would relieve a particular family from being forced to seek financial aid from the parish, or being driven to find shelter in almshouses or workhouses.[31]

In present-day Wales, a social function centred around food and drink is still regarded as one of the most effective methods of raising money for social aid. In addition to the national and international charities who appeal for financial support, there are many causes in our country that are strictly of Welsh concern. Providing an effective nursery-education system through the medium of the Welsh language demands constant monetary support throughout the whole of the country. Social evenings are organized regularly, both in private houses and in public community centres to raise money for the local nursery school. In the rural areas, a coffee evening always proves successful, attenders pay a fixed sum for a cup of coffee and light refreshment which usually consists of a few savoury delicacies and home-made cakes.

Attenders are also invited to contribute items towards a food-stall, and the sale of home-made fruit-breads, cakes and preserves during the evening always comes up to expectation. Similar functions are organized in urban districts, but the cheese-and-wine party seems to have superseded the coffee evening in the more sophisticated circles. Open-air barbecues are also favoured in both rural and coastal regions during the summer months, the rural communities being more ambitious in this respect. Whole beasts are roasted, as in former times, and the first slices from the oxen are auctioned to set the standard price for the evening. Sausages and beefburgers are the more ordinary fare provided at the less formal barbecue.

In conclusion, some general themes have emerged in the consideration of food as a means of social communication in Wales. When discussing living in underprivileged circumstances through the centuries, food must be recognized in the context of 'eating to live'. Living through periods of hardship made people more aware of their fellow-beings' needs and welfare. Carrying out major tasks without mechanical aid also forces people to be dependent on one another for practical help, a system which promoted congenial community spirit. Contributions to ease hardship or as a reward for help, as already discussed, were usually expressed by gifts of food, which varied according to individual means and resources. To the recipients, extra provisions or an invitation to partake of a meal outside the home relieved their own domestic food supplies. Good hospitality also ruled at all times. The necessity of eating to live also inspired people to use food as a social aid. In modern times, paying for good-quality food is a pleasant experience which can be regarded as an 'investment' for the consumer. In turn, the monetary transaction brings aid to support the charitable cause. Indeed, both directly and indirectly, food promotes communication between all members of society in order to sustain life.

NOTES

[1] Sir Richard Colt Hoare, Bart (ed.), *The Itinerary of Archbishop Baldwin through Wales* by Gerald de Bari (London, 1806), vol. 2, p.292.

[2] David Jenkins, *The Agricultural Community of South-West Wales* (Cardiff, 1971), pp.83–4.

[3] Huw Evans, *The Gorse Glen* (Liverpool, 1948), pp.47–8.

[4] Jenkins, *The Agricultural Community of South-West Wales*, p.99.

[5] Thomas Pennant, *Tours in Wales* (London, 1810), vol.II, pp.276–7.

[6] George Borrow, *Wild Wales* (London, 1901), pp.219–20.

[7] Hugh Owen, *The Life and Works of Lewis Morris (1701–1765)* (1951), p.142.

[8] W. Maddock Williams, 'A slight historical and topographical sketch of the parish of Llanfechain', *Montgomeryshire Collections*, 5 (1872), 203–84.

[9] *Bye-gones*, 24 January 1894.

[10] *Bye-gones*, 2 December 1981.

[11] D. Roy Saer, 'The Christmas carol-singing tradition in the Tanad valley', *Folk Life*, 7 (1969), 15–42.

[12] D. G. Williams, 'Casgliad o lên gwerin Sir Gaerfyrddin', *Transactions of National Eisteddfod of Wales* (Llanelli, 1895), pp.288–9.

[13] D. Parry Jones, *Welsh Country Upbringing* (London, 1948), p.61.

[14] Trefor M. Owen, *Welsh Folk Customs* (Cardiff, 1968), p.146.

[15] Evans, *The Gorse Glen*, pp.50–1.

[16] Mary Curtis, *The Antiquities of Laugharne, Pendine and their Neighbourhoods* (1880), pp.210–11.

[17] Owen, *Welsh Folk Customs*, p.44.

[18] Ibid., p.45.

[19] Frances Hoggan, 'Notes on Welsh folk-lore', *Folk-lore* (1893), p.122.

[20] Stephen J. Williams and J. Enoch Powell, *Cyfreithiau Hywel Dda yn ôl Llyfr Blegywryd* (Cardiff, 1942), p.69.

[21] Curtis, *The Antiquities of Laugharne, Pendine and their Neigbourhoods*, pp.210–11.

[22] Wirt Sikes, *Rambles and Studies in Old South Wales* (1881), p.53.

[23] Walter Haydn Davies, *Blithe Ones* (Port Talbot, 1979), p.20.

[24] J. Geraint Jenkins, 'Cockles and mussels: aspects of shellfish gathering in Wales', *Folk Life*, 15 (1977), 81–95.

[25] S. Minwel Tibbott, *Welsh Fare* (Cardiff, 1976), p.68.

[26] Curtis, *The Antiquities of Laugharne, Pendine and their Neigbourhoods*, pp. 210–11.

[27] D. E. Jones, *Hanes Plwyfi Llangeler a Phenboyr* (Llandysul, 1897), pp.368–9.

[28] D. G. Williams, 'Casgliad o lên gwerin Sir Gaerfyrddin', pp.287–8.

[29] Tibbott, *Welsh Fare*, p.20.

[30] Owen, *Welsh Folk Customs*, p.166.

[31] Fred S. Price, *History of Llansawel* (Swansea, 1898), p.8; R. M. Evans, 'Folklore and customs in Cardiganshire', *Cardiganshire Antiquarian Society Transactions*, 12 (1937), 55; D. G. Williams, 'Casgliad o lên gwerin Sir Gaerfyrddin', p.288.

Laundering in the Welsh Home

One of the earliest accounts of washing clothes is that found in the *Odyssey* of Homer, thought to have originated in the eighth century BC. The scene depicts Nausikäa, the princess of the Phaiakins, and her maids on an island:

> Now when they had come to the delightful stream of the river, where there was always a washing place, and plenty of glorious water, that ran through the wash what was ever so dirty, there, they unyoked the mules . . . while they, from the wagon, lifted the wash in their hands and carried it to the black water, and stamped on it in the basins, making a race and game of it, until they had washed and rinsed all dirt away – then spread it out in line along the beach of the sea, where the water of the sea had washed the most pebbles up on the dry shore. Then they themselves, after bathing and anointing themselves with olive oil ate their dinner all along by the banks of the river and waited for the laundry to dry out in the sunshine.[1]

No doubt, the principles of washing fabrics have remained constant ever since men and women have been wearing clothes or have used bedclothes. Basically, the sequence has not changed throughout the centuries – the primitive method of washing in a river or tub, treading or pounding with a stone or wooden bat, rinsing, followed by a crude form of mangling is evident in the programme carried out by the most sophisticated of washing machines today. However, fabrics have been developed in each country according to the available indigenous materials to meet the climate. It is known that the countries of western Europe, including those of Great Britain, used more wool than cotton, linen or other fabrics until the end of the Middle Ages.

The men in Roman Britain wore a loincloth of wool or linen knotted around the waist, over which they wore a tunic made of woollen material of varying weights. White was their favourite colour, while the poorer men wore garments of unbleached wool. The women's tunics, like those for the men, were also made of wool or linen.[2] At this period, the fullers were responsible for cleaning soiled garments as well as treating newly woven clothes. They were first placed in vats and washed in soda and water, treated with fuller's earth, and then, if white, they were spread out on wicker frames over a pot of burning sulphur for bleaching. Next, they were washed again, hung out to dry, and then pressed in clothes presses while still slightly damp. No detailed account survives of all these processes, but sculptures and paintings from France and Italy show slaves treading on the clothes in the vats and workmen bringing the wicker cages and pot of sulphur for bleaching. Fullers had to replace any goods which were stolen or gnawed by mice. They also had to pay up if a slave brought home the wrong laundry.[3]

Finding references to clothes worn in Wales in the Middle Ages is not difficult, but accounts regarding their care for the same period are negligible. In the early medieval period, the tales of the Mabinogion offer detailed descriptions of dress, for example a maiden dressed in a silk vest with clasps of gold, a surcoat of gold tissue, a frontlet of gold upon her head, with rubies, gems and pearls. These were obviously instances of royal apparel. The horsemen in the story of Pwyll, prince of Dyfed, were 'clad in garments of grey woollen' which was a more ordinary form of dress. Gerallt Gymro (Giraldus Cambrensis) in 1188, when journeying through Wales with Archbishop Baldwin, noted that the dress of the Welshman was 'a thin mantle and shirt only, worn both by day and night'. The Laws of Hywel Dda, codified in the tenth century, also mention costumes of linen and wool, but the only hint as to their care is a reference to the *golchures* (the washerwoman) and *golchbren* (a washing bat).

Due to the absence of earlier documentary evidence, this study will of necessity concentrate mainly on the history of laundering in the Welsh home from the eighteenth century to the early twentieth century. The evidence for the later years of the nineteenth and early twentieth century will be based, to a large extent, on oral testimony collected widely from experienced, elderly informants.

Seventeenth-century household account books for English country houses show that the 'cycle of the buck' (see p.29), or the regularity of washday, varied enormously at that time. In a few households clothes were washed once a fortnight, but once a month or even once a quarter was more common. Sometimes the 'buck' coincided with the departure of a family from its town house to its country seat or vice versa. Gladys Scott Thomson, writing of the Bedford family in July 1675 at Woburn, after the duke's family had departed from London, recorded:[4]

> For washing sheets and napkins before the great wash when the two masters were in town   2s. 0d.
> For three women one day to wash   4s. 6d.

At Bedford House, London similar preparations took place:

> For soap for the great wash when the family left for London   4s. 6d.
> For two women to wash after his lordship's being in town   3s. 0d.

At Chirk Castle, the seat of Sir Richard Myddleton on the English–Welsh border, a similar reference is found in the Household Accounts for the year 1684:

> Paid Jayne Browne, the waisherwoman for waishinge 43 dozens of napkins at 4d. per dozen soe agreed with Mrs Kynaston, 14/4d. and XIId. for washing yor owne cloath when the Dukes of Ormond and Beauford were at the Castle.[5]

During the nineteenth century, infrequent washdays were still recommended in certain housekeeping manuals. They stressed that it was both more convenient and more economical to save up dirty linen and wash a large number of items at one time. In 1838, for instance, *The Workman's Guide* advised: 'it is best economy to wash by the year or by the quarter, in places where it can be done, and by the score or dozen in preference to the piece'.

As a result, the practice of infrequent washing became a status symbol, for only the well-to-do families could afford sufficient clothing to make it possible. Infrequent washdays were indicative not of slovenly habits, but of affluence. In the 1890s Miss Lane, the postmistress of Candleford Green 'still kept to the old middle-class custom of one huge washing of linen every 6 weeks. In her girlhood, it would have been thought poor-looking to have had a weekly or fortnightly washday.'[6]

Eighteenth-century household account books of country mansions in Wales, however, throw a different light on the washday pattern in rural Wales at this period. The detailed Household Account Book for the years 1763–83 for Edwinsford, the Williams's seat in north Carmarthenshire, includes regular weekly payments for washing, for example '15 Nov. 1763 – pd. For washing 3d., 22 Nov. 1763 pd. 2 weemen for washing 6d.' etc.[7] Similar references are found in the Account Book of Noyadd Llanarth (Cardiganshire) for 1793–1805. It notes a weekly payment for 'washing – 3d. . . . washing and brewing 6d.' and occasionally refers to the washerwoman in person, for example 'paid Sara Moris for was[h]ing 6d.'[8] These weekly washdays in such households (the estate of Edwinsford at this date encompassed 10,700 acres), should not be interpreted as an indication of poverty, but rather point to the absence of facilities to cope with the washing of a large number of items at longer intervals.

In this context, it is appropriate to discuss briefly the facilities for washing or laundering in different types of household. References to a laundry as a specific room, even in the larger country houses, are sparse before the eighteenth century. The earliest reference found, to date, is to the purchasing of necessary items for the laundry in the household of Henry Percy, the ninth earl of Northumberland. Among the sundry purchases for his lordship's house and affairs were 'lynes for the laundry' and '11 kettles for the laundrye' paid from the general account for 1597–8.[9] An inventory for probate of the earl's goods in 1632–3 also lists the items found in the laundry, which reads

'Item – one livory bedsted, matt and corde, one feather bedd and boulster, one grey rugg and one paire of blanketts'.[10] This may suggest that the room was also used as a bedroom.

Examination of late seventeenth- and early eighteenth-century inventories for country mansions in Wales by and large has shown the absence of references to a laundry while the contents of the kitchen, buttery, dairy, cellar or malt room were regularly listed. The inventories examined were for Hengwrt (1696), Plas Brondanw (1712), both in Merioneth, and Bodwrda, Aberdaron, on the Llŷn Peninsula (1705). On the other hand, an item in the accounts of the household of an Anglesey gentleman, Henry Morgan of Henblas (1734), hints at the existence of a laundry there. It simply states that the laundry was equipped 'with 2 Box Irons and 8 Flat Irons'.[11] The house at Erddig, Denbighshire (built between 1684 and 1687 for Joshua Edisbury, the high sheriff of the county), when extended by a later owner in 1774, was equipped with a wet laundry, a dry laundry and a laundry yard. A significant entry into the Household Accounts Book for Edwinsford again, for 13 August 1777, refers to the payment of 'a washerwoman in ye laundry' in contrast to the payment made to 'ye woman who washed in ye house' on the same day. Entries for paying a washer-woman between 1763 and 1777 do not refer to the laundry, but regular payments after this date cover washing and mangling in the laundry.[12]

By the early nineteenth century, however, it is easier to prove that the larger Welsh country houses were provided with a laundry, consisting of a wash-house, together with an ironing and drying room in some instances. An early nineteenth-century inventory for the Mansion House at Llysnewydd in the parish of Llangeler, Carmarthenshire, for example, specified the contents of the laundry there, namely '1 mangle by Baker, 1 Iron stone and flews, 2 Deal Tables, 2 small ditto, 4 Clothes Baskets, 1 large trunk, 4 Cloathes Horses, 1 Box, 2 Box and Heaters, 4 Iron Stands, 3 Tin canisters. Sundry Lanthorns'.[13] By the second half of the nineteenth century many large farmhouses had emulated the country mansions by building what was usually known as the boiler house (tŷ pair) or brewhouse (briws), equipped with an iron furnace or boiler for heating the water. Washing in smaller farmhouses, country cottages and terraced houses in the industrial valleys, however, was confined to the kitchen or scullery, but it was general custom on a dry summer's day to place the washtub outdoors in the backyard. The only means of heating the water would be cast-iron boilers, kettles or zinc buckets suspended over the open fire in the kitchen. This situation remained unchanged well into the twentieth century.

MATERIALS AND EQUIPMENT

Water
A very high percentage of houses in Wales, even in the early decades of the twentieth century, did not have an indoor supply of piped water. In the

agricultural areas it would be carried in pitchers or buckets from the nearest stream or well and stored in tubs and barrels. When carrying water from a considerable distance, many informants referred to the advantage of using a wooden yoke as an aid, the weight being evenly distributed across the shoulders, thus relieving the strain on the arms and wrists. Larger farms would use a horse-drawn sled to transport a greater volume in large barrels. An alternative method, practised in rural areas, especially in the summer months, was to carry the soiled garments together with the wash-tub and cast-iron boiler to the nearest stream. With a fire lit in a sheltered position nearby, and a plentiful supply of water at hand, the whole operation of washing and rinsing would be carried out without too much effort. This method was still practised periodically in the early twentieth century, in the districts of Llansannan and Gwytherin in Denbighshire, in the Llanwrtyd district of Breconshire and in the rural areas near Pont-rhyd-y-fen in Glamorgan. In the industrial areas, a communal tap would serve many terraces in the villages, but scattered households in both the coal-mining and slate-quarrying districts also would have to carry their supply of water from a stream or well. Informants from all areas spoke of the special attribute of rainwater for washing: its softness was an aid to lathering and all efforts were made to store it in barrels.

Fuller's Earth and Lye

Clothes were cleaned in fulling mills with fuller's earth and alkali. The former absorbed fat, the latter formed soluble compounds with it. The alkali usually employed was urine that had become ammoniacal, but sometimes lye from wood ash was used. The action of these substances was aided by mechanical beating in the fulling mills and they remained in use until the end of the Middle Ages. Isolated references to their use at a later period, even when soap had become commercially available, are found in eighteenth-century Welsh household account books. Elizabeth Martin of Vervil, Coity Lower, Bridgend (Glamorgan) has one entry for 'Fullersearth 6d., Soap 3d.' for 12 September 1763.[14] The Edwinsford Account Book contains a similar reference to paying 'the washerwoman for foulers earth, 6d.' on 1 January 1771.[15]

Lye, that is, alkalized water, was also used for washing clothes. Made basically from oak or beech ashes, mixed in boiling water with slaked lime and human or animal urine, the process was complicated and there were many boilings and strainings. A reference to payment for ashes used in washing is found in the Chirk Castle Account Book for 8 December 1665: 'Paid Jane Brown for ashes that went to waish the children's clothes'.[16] Soap remained expensive until the second half of the nineteenth century and many households were forced to use soap substitutes to eke out their soap supply. An informant from Gyffylliog (Denbighshire) recalled how her maternal grandmother would collect a quantity of sheep's dung, to which she would add boiling water and then allow it to stand overnight. This provided her with an effective soap-jelly. It is known that soap substitutes were also made from household grease and from wood ash or urine-based lye. Oral evidence confirms that it was common practice to use urine as an aid for washing clothes. The Welsh noun *golch*, the common word used in north Wales for urine, is homonymic with the general Welsh term *golch* for a 'washing'. One informant reported a washerwoman in Denbighshire who stored sour urine in a container, and added a specific measure of the ammoniacal fluid to ordinary soap-water when washing white linens. Informants from south and west Wales confirmed that their mothers adhered to this practice when washing white garments.

Soap

In the context of this study, the history of soap manufacture and its availability as a commercial product in Wales before the eighteenth century has not been looked at in any detail. However, it is of interest to note that in 1711 a levy of a penny a pound was added to the price of soap, a very heavy levy for that period, and most ordinary households were forced to continue with the custom of making their own supply. Soap-making with wood ash and tallow was a simple but tedious task. A recipe in the hand of Meryell Williams of Ystumcolwyn, found in an early eighteenth-century Welsh manuscript, gives detailed instructions for using two bushels of fern or wood ash to one peck of limestone to provide the lye required to boil with twenty-four pounds of tallow. The whole process took some four days to complete.[17]

The tax on soap was abolished in 1853 and consumption per head in Britain rose steadily from 3.6lb per annum in 1801 to 8lb per annum in 1861.[18] By 1891 it had nearly doubled, and local soap chandlers provided the required supply. For example, Thomas Davies, the Chandlery, Trealaw in the Rhondda valley (Glamorgan), supplied the district with a yellow primrose soap, a cheap brown soap for scouring and also a red carbolic soap.[19] By this period a regular purchasing pattern for soap is evident. An Account Book of a rural store in Crwbin (Carmarthenshire) for 1881 shows, for example, that one David Griffiths (Never) purchased on '1 October – Soap 4d., on 5 October – Soap 4d., Blue – 1d., soda – 1d.'[20] Similar entries for specific customers occur regularly. Another rural store in Hendre Cwm-main, in the heart of Merioneth, for 1898–9 confirms the same pattern; for example, one Lewis Jones, Brynnau, purchased on '12 November 1898, soap 3d., drei sop ½d., 9 January 1899, soap 8d., drei soap 1d.'[21]

These two examples point to the materials available to the housewife at this time to facilitate the process of washing, namely, soap, dry soap, soda and blue. Informants describe the soap as ordinary household soap, pale yellow, bought in bars some two to three feet long (*sebon bar, calan o sebon*). Cut into smaller blocks it was stored before use in soap nets or wire baskets, which were suspended from the kitchen ceiling. Air was allowed to circulate around it freely to make it harder and more concentrated. 'As hard as stone or bone' was the usual simile quoted, and the older informants were of the same firm opinion that hardness promoted frugality. The soap was usually rubbed directly on to the soiled garments. The branded Naphtha and Carbolic soaps were also mentioned when treating workmen's clothes. The introduction of a powdered soap came with the 'dry soap' (Hudson's was the brand quoted) and informants were of the unanimous opinion that it was a welcome aid. A small quantity dissolved in hot water provided them with a soap-sud solution which was then augmented by rubbing the bar-soap on heavily soiled areas. Informants who recalled the introduction of luxury, branded aids such as Rinso and Lux reported that their mothers were reluctant to use them. They refused to be victims of such extravagance.

Bleaching Agents

Bleaching agents were also accepted as washing aids by the late nineteenth century, and informants constantly referred to the use of common washing soda and 'blue' for bleaching white linen and cotton items. Soda was also regarded as a water softener. Nineteenth-century housekeeping manuals promoted the use of borax or saltpetre as bleaching agents and maintained that they were less injurious to fabrics than soda.[22] However, informants were not familiar with their use in this context.

Blue

Blue, a compound bought in a solid block and tied in a linen bag, was employed regularly; dipped in a tubful of clean water and squeezed gently, it provided a sky-blue solution which was used as the final rinsing water for the white garments. Care was taken not to make the solution too strong as this would give an unsightly grey colour to the clothes. Informants from rural areas also testified to the excellent attributes of a freshly mown hay-meadow for bleaching white garments. White twill or calico sheets when new would be washed and spread out evenly on clean grass and left there for a few days to bleach. This treatment also proved effective for removing stubborn stains from white tablecloths. A green hedge was proved to have similar bleaching qualities and many informants were of the firm opinion that frosty air enhanced whiteness.

Starch

Starch was another aid that was used to improve the appearance of certain garments. In the Elizabethan period, ruffs and headdresses were stiffened with wires and size mixtures, but it is thought that starch was introduced into England by a Dutch lady, Mistress Dingham of Flanders, in 1554. It is recorded that she introduced the art of starching to England and that she and some of her compatriots set up a school for teaching laundresses 'the arts of folding, pleating, starching and the making of starch'.[23] Starch is obtained in varying proportions from all vegetables, but that from rice or wheat was most generally used for laundry work. Laundresses maintained that by stiffening the garments, starch not only improved the appearance of clothes but also helped to keep them clean for a longer period.

Oral testimony proved that starch was used widely in all areas at the turn of the century, and informants described two different types of starch solutions prepared in most homes. A hot-water starch would be used for treating ordinary household items such as table linen, pillowcases and aprons. After preparing a thin, transparent solution, all items would be immersed in it, wrung and then put out to dry. A cold-water starch would be employed for stiffening collars, cuffs, shirt-fronts or any other article requiring a very stiff finish. A fairly thick, cold solution would be prepared, in which the individual items were carefully immersed. Then they were rolled tightly in a clean, dry cloth and kept damp for ironing. Cold-water starching demanded great skill and the ironing of the treated garments had to be executed with painstaking care. White collars and shirt-fronts, worn regularly by the menfolk, were usually reserved and treated separately from the ordinary household wash. Certain ladies were known to regard the whole operation as a special craft, and in most villages an 'expert' would be available to relieve the ordinary housewife of this task. In turn, the 'expert' would welcome the monetary reward gained in this way.

Bucks

Bucks or wooden tubs are always prominent in early engravings or paintings depicting a washday. The noun 'buck' is defined in the *Oxford English Dictionary* as a 'washing tub, a vat in which to steep clothes in lye'; referring to the 'buck' or 'bucking' as the periodic 'great wash' is a secondary use of the same noun. Coopered tubs of various diameters and depths were general-purpose vessels made by local craftsmen and were used in most houses for brewing and other general tasks such as washing clothes. Seventeenth- and eighteenth-century inventories of the household goods of country mansions in Wales include regular references to 'wooden vessels in ye cellar' or to 'barrels and hogsheads', but specific references to washing tubs or bucking tubs are rare. However, an inventory of the Goods of Pencreek, Llanhennock (Monmouthshire) as left in 1698, specified that 'in the Kill [were] . . . 2 Great Malt Vats and 3 bucking tubs'.[24] Also the goods of Penry Vaughan, Llether Llyesty (Carmarthenshire) on 29 December 1716 included 'a washing tub, kneading trough, andirons, an old balance and spit – valued at 3/-'.[25] A stanza found in an eighteenth-century manuscript in the hand of Richard Morris of Anglesey not only refers to the wooden tub, but also depicts the whole scene of washing on the river bank.

> Mae yn yr afon grwcc yngwluch
> A chylcha gwuch o onnen.[26]
>
> [In the river is a wooden tub, steeping,
> With excellent bands of ash.]

An oak wash-tub was regarded as an essential item of a young bride's dowry in the later decades of the nineteenth century, and it is evident from oral testimony that Welsh housewives had not abandoned the wooden tub at the turn of the twentieth century. Usually they used wooden barrels or hogsheads sawn in two halves. Most of the informants, however, recalled the intro-duction of the ribbed, galvanized dolly tub and the zinc trough or bath. The latter seems to have superseded the wooden tub in most districts by the late 1930s, whereas the dolly tub was generally reserved for washing heavy items, especially in the industrial areas.

Bats

A washing bat (*golchbren*) was an aid used originally when washing clothes in a river or stream. The clothes were placed on a stone or rock and beaten clean with a wooden bat. An early reference to *golchbren* is found in the Laws of Hywel Dda, namely, '*naud er holchuryes hyd y burhyo ay golchbren*' (the laundress . . . her protection is as far as she can throw her dolly).[27] References are also found in seventeenth- and eighteenth-century Welsh texts as in the final couplet of the following stanza:

> Ag ar y garreg olchi heb go
> Rwi yn tybio gado yr golchbren.[28]

> [And on the washing stone, forgetful,
> I suspect that I have left the washing bat.]

This confirms its use in conjunction with the washing stone.

Nineteenth-century washing bats from the collections of the Museum of Welsh Life.

A woman hitting a man with a washing bat is carved on an oak misericord of 1401 in Carlisle cathedral, and an illustration in a Harleian manuscript of 1582 shows that early washing bats were shovel-shaped with short, wide blades.[29] Edward Pinto states that later models were made from various hardwoods, in one piece, and in one of two forms. They were carved with a plain face with bevels on both edges at the back of the blade, or with a cross-ribbed face which could also act as a rubbing board.[30] Examples of both types have been donated to the Museum of Welsh Life, but oral evidence regarding their use is sparse. One inform-ant, writing of washing customs in the Llanwrtyd Wells district of Breconshire in the second half of the nineteenth century, reported that they were employed when washing blankets on the river bank in early summer.

Washing Dolly

A washing dolly was a logical development from the bat. Given the general name of dolly, as it was regarded as resembling a doll, it was also known in different parts of Britain as dolly pin, poss stick or peggy stick. Basically a nineteenth-century implement, it consists of an upright turned pole of ash or elm, through which passes a turned cross-bar handle. At its lower end, the pole fits into a circular beech 'stool' with four, five or six turned 'legs'. Another type is fitted with a wooden dome with high arches cut through from each side, which was again replaced by a third type, a metal cone, usually copper, with louvres in its sides. Both wooden types were used widely throughout Wales and were operated in the wooden or zinc tubs; the plunging, stirring, pounding actions assisted in working the soapy water through the clothes and in ridding them of dirt. Their use, however, by the early decades of the twentieth century, seems to have been restricted to the handling of heavy items such as

Examples of different types of washing dolly, from the collections of the Museum of Welsh Life.

blankets and quilts. The lighter, metal-cone type, generally known as *stompar* or *pwnner*, does not seem to have had such a wide distribution, but a plain wooden stick, also given the same alternative names, was used in many districts for plunging clothes when being boiled during the course of the wash.

Washing Board

It seems that the dolly was made redundant with the introduction of the washing board or scrubbing board. A ribbed, wooden board in a wooden frame with the vertical bars extended to form two legs is believed to have originated in Scandinavia, and its manufacture then spread to other countries during the nineteenth century.[31] A board patented in the 1830s was advertised as saving soap and as having a 'sanitary front drain'.[32] The wooden board, in turn, was superseded by a metal board of galvanized zinc or brass with draining holes, and lastly by a glass board. Oral evidence points to an even distribution of wash-boards in use throughout Wales in the early decades of the twentieth century, the majority of them being brass or zinc. A few informants had witnessed the use of a wooden board as a forerunner to the metal one and others testified to the introduction of the glass board as a modern version of the metal type. Known as *golchwr, styllen olchi, pren golchi* or *bord golchi* in north Wales and as *rwber, borden olchi* or *morwn*

Miss Kate John, Merthyr Tydfil, using a washboard for washing clothes, 1940s.

olchi in south Wales, it seems to have been in general use with the wider galvanized-zinc pan or bath, although some informants recalled that it was employed in the more restricted wooden tub. Being lighter than the dolly to handle, it was regarded by informants as an excellent aid for washing heavily soiled garments; when laid on the board, the soiled area would be covered with soap and then briskly rubbed against the ribbed surface to loosen the dirt. This procedure relieved the hands of the unaided, vigorous rubbing and expedited the whole operation of washing.

Washing Machines

Washing machines were available from the late eighteenth century, and many nineteenth-century models were based on the principle of friction, incorporating mechanical versions of the traditional dolly and scrubbing board. They were introduced into some Welsh homes late in the nineteenth century when they became readily available on the market, but informants in general were sceptical of their harsh, mechanical actions with the possible ill-treatment of fabrics. They were also deemed to increase soap consumption, and another prohibitive factor was the informant's own prejudice that machines did not wash as cleanly as the traditional manual methods. Undoubtedly, oral evidence proves that the wash-tub and board method was still used in most homes until after the Second World War.

THE WASHING

Given the facilities, the materials and the equipment already discussed, the general method adopted to contend with the family wash seems to have followed a similar pattern throughout Wales. Minor digressions were perceived, but oral evidence, collected widely, provides us with a basic pattern. Clothes or garments were divided into specific categories and the washing followed a strict pattern. The first wash dealt with all white articles only, then came the coloured items, followed by the woollen garments and, finally, the fourth category included all the dirtier, rougher items such as socks, stockings, sack-aprons and dusters.

The white garments – that is, all the linen and cotton items – formed a major part of the weekly wash and were usually given special treatment. Having been washed in the first water, they were rinsed, wrung and placed in a second tub. They were then well covered with soap before being put into a suitable receptacle for boiling. Soda was added to the water and they were boiled for some twenty minutes. Afterwards, they were rinsed in clean water, wrung and again immersed in the final blue-water bleach. Selected items were also dipped in a hot-water starch solution at this last stage. Finally, they were wrung and were ready then for drying.

Coloured items, such as cotton prints, aprons and so on, were given a straight-forward washing, rubbing and rinsing treatment, but care was taken not to add soda to the water as this would cause loss of colour. Flannel shirts, petticoats and drawers also formed a large proportion of the family wash and they needed great care. Hot water caused them to shrink and discolour, while rubbing, wringing and over-handling caused the fibres to felt or matt. Informants stressed that a lukewarm soapy water should be used, and that successful results depended on gentle handling, drawing the garment up and down in the water fairly quickly. Rinsed thoroughly and carefully twice or three times in cold water (although some informants preferred using lukewarm water), each garment should be wrung gently, given a good shake and then hung out to dry.

Occupational clothes formed another category and it was the general custom to allocate a separate day for washing them, usually towards the end of the working week. Agricultural workers usually wore a flannel shirt and corduroy trousers. The corduroy trousers were washed regularly and required special treatment. Soaked overnight and washed in soapy water, they were scrubbed with an ordinary scrubbing brush. Laid evenly on a flat surface, usually on a stone slab outside the house, they were scrubbed in one direction only, following the grain of the cloth, and then were rinsed thoroughly, preferably in running water in a nearby stream or spring. Originally the trousers would be dark brown in colour, but with frequent washing and scrubbing it was inevitable that they would fade and become white. The farmers, however, bore some prejudice against wearing light-coloured corduroy trousers, and, accordingly, informants in the rural districts of west Denbighshire practised an ingenious method of restoring the original colour. Boiling a ball of hay in water provided them with a suitable dye in which the trousers were immersed after the final rinse. The trousers were then drip-dried to ensure even drying.

Corduroy trousers and a fustian or linen jacket formed the basic garments of the slate-quarry workers' occupational dress. In this community, tradition demanded that, when clean, both trousers and jacket were to be a brilliant white. In this instance, the original brown or grey trousers had to be scrubbed white and every housewife strove to provide the menfolk with a brilliant white outfit for the first Monday of every month. A slate slab (*stelin*) was fitted in most backyards to provide a suitable surface to facilitate outdoor washing and scrubbing.

Coal-miners wore dark-coloured flannel shirts and their trousers were made of moleskin (a cotton fustian) or duck (a lightweight linen texture). Both materials were proved to be hard wearing. Informants again recalled a similar procedure for washing these items.

The washing of blankets and quilts was a seasonal operation carried out in the spring or summer months. Specific references to this task are found in eighteenth-century household account books; for example, an entry for 9 May 1776 in the Edwinsford Account Book reads: 'Paid two women 1 day washing quilts and blankets 8d.' A similar entry is found for 15 June 1783. The Noyadd Llanarth Account Book also includes the following entries for 31 August 1795 and 10 August 1798, 'for washing blankets 1/6d.' In this context, it was found that in rural areas they adhered to the primitive custom of washing alongside a river or stream. Demanding a large quantity of water, the task was made easier by carrying all the other requisites and appliances to the riverside. A fire would be lit nearby and the blankets washed in a tub. Rubbed gently with ordinary bar-soap, they would be washed twice in lukewarm water and finally rinsed in cold water, either in the tub or in the stream. Evidence of this method practised at the turn of the century was given in specific areas in Cardiganshire, Denbighshire and Breconshire. The same method was adopted when washing in a tub, either in the house or backyard. After a thorough rinsing, the heavy blankets would be wrung. This task demanded the strength of two persons, each holding the blanket at one end and twisting it in opposite directions to rid it of excess water. Most informants reported also that they would proceed to shake the blanket after wringing, to restore its fluffy texture and thus preventing it from matting when drying.

DRYING

The general methods adopted for drying all garments were governed to some degree by geographical conditions as well as traditional practices. In exposed rural areas, of high altitude, the inhabitants were forced to spread all garments on low-lying bushes and hedges. Gorse bushes were classed superior to thorn hedges, they were not as prickly and thus were not so prone to tear the clothes. They also allowed the wind to blow through them freely, to accelerate drying. Wind direction was also considered and informants emphasized that the clothes were always spread out so that the wind blew directly on them and therefore they were not in danger of being blown away. In the absence of gorse bushes, thorn hedges would be trimmed so that the thorns grew inward into the heart of the hedge, making the surface less injurious to the garments. In very exposed areas, however, heather bushes were used wherever possible; they provided the housewife with excellent, low drying patches as well as pleasantly perfumed garments.

In low-lying areas, most households in the early decades of the twentieth century were proud owners of a clothes line. It would consist of a length of wire secured between two posts some seven feet high, usually positioned in a nearby orchard or field. The garments would be held in position with pegs, and the height and tension of the line could be adjusted by a third post, slightly forked, known as a clothes prop. However, informants referred to the regular use of the hedge to take the overspill from the line, more especially the lighter, rougher garments. They also adhered to the practice of spreading white garments on a newly mown field in the summer months: to retain the whiteness of laundered garments was a virtue, the mark of a good housewife, and constant bleaching on the grass kept them 'as white as snow' ('mor wyn â'r eira').

In the industrial areas of both north and south Wales, lines were used in preference to hedges or bushes, but informants there were also aware of old practices. However, the coal-miners' wives were faced with the hazard of coal dust contaminating the atmosphere. When living within a certain distance of a working pit, the drying periods were restricted to certain intervals between work shifts.

Both the rural and industrial communities were without special facilities for indoor drying. During prolonged periods of wet weather, however, clothes-lines, racks or clothes-horses would be erected in the kitchen.

Mangles

Linen, cotton and other fabrics, having been washed and dried, had to be made smooth by mangling and ironing. The dry garments would be dampened, folded and rolled tightly in preparation for these final processes. An eighteenth-century housekeeping manual points out that a mangle was a device for making household linen smooth. This definition is confirmed by that given in the *Oxford English Dictionary*, namely: 'a machine for rolling and pressing linen and cotton clothing etc.' One of the earliest mangles, widely distributed in western and northern Europe, was a hand mangle. It comprised simply a flat, wooden board approximately thirty inches long by six inches wide and half an inch thick, and a wooden roller approximately eighteen to twenty-four inches long. The undersurface or working surface of the board and that of the roller had to be perfectly smooth. The mangling was performed by wrapping the damp garment around the roller, placing it on a table and working the roller to and fro by means of the board, the one hand grasping the handle or top end, while the other pressed downwards on the back of the board.

Both Welsh and English mangle boards were generally plain, but Dutch and Norwegian examples had elaborate ornamentation. The pattern on the upper surface was usually of a geometrical, scroll or floral design, with the initials of the owner and the date of carving invariably incorporated into the decoration. Similar examples were also found in Scotland. Some Norwegian boards were carved with a handle, often bearing zoomorphic designs in the form of a horse. All hand mangles were eventually superseded by the flat or sad-iron.

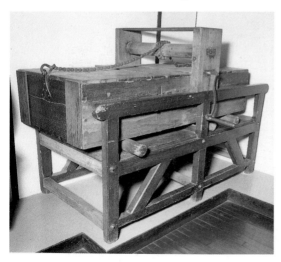

An early nineteenth-century box mangle (approximately 178 cm long by 140 cm high).

Box mangles were invented by the seventeenth century and it is known that, in 1696, the duchess of Hamilton received a mangle from her cousin, the countess of Rothes. This was bought for £53 (Scot.) and sent to Edinburgh with the wheelwright who was to show the laundrywomen how it worked.[33] In an eighteenth-century trade directory the early manufacturers of mangles included Baker and Son of Fore Street, Joseph Hampson of Smithfield and J. T. Oxenham of Oxford Street.[34] It was noted that '1 mangle by Baker' was listed as an item in the laundry of the Mansion House at Llysnewydd, Llangeler in 1828.[35] An earlier reference to a mangle, made by a craftsman, is found in the household account book of Golden Grove, the seat of the Vaughans in Carmarthenshire –

'Travelling craftsmen often called – David Morris received £4 for making a mangle in 1789'.[36] References to employing local labour for operating a mangle are also found in the Edwinsford Account Book, for example on 6 May 1776: 'Paid to the clothiers dauther to helpe mangle all the household linen. 4 days, 1s. 4d.' Regular references to paying a woman 4d. at mangling appear in this account book after 1777.[37]

The box, usually of oak, would be filled with stones, and the total weight was said to be nearly a ton. The weighted box ran backward and forward over the loose rollers, around which the clothes were wound. Smaller pieces were folded inside larger items such as sheets and tablecloths. When the box had reached the end of its travel in each direction, it automatically tipped so that the rollers could be removed and the mangled clothes replaced by another lot. Only two rollers were mangled at any one time, while the third was being clothed. The box would be driven by a rope, a leather strap or a chain.

Cast-iron upright mangle outside the 1925 Rhyd-y-car cottage, Museum of Welsh Life.

These large, ponderous mangles, found only in larger houses, were superseded gradually by the much smaller, spring-loaded wringing and mangling machine. With adjustable rollers, this machine could be adapted for both wringing and mangling. It consisted of two rollers, one above the other, fitted on a heavy cast-iron stand, the wooden rollers rotated by a large wheel and the pressure adjusted by a screw. Plain Brown Holland mangling cloths, supplied by the mangle-maker, were wrapped around the clothes before they were pressed through the rollers. These cloths provided the garments with the required glossy finish.

With the advent of these machines, another cottage industry affiliated to washing was developed. Public sympathy for a wife whose husband was incapacitated or killed by a mining or quarrying accident frequently took the form of a subscription list to purchase a mangle, with which she could earn a living. A classic example, representing the custom in the slate-quarrying villages of north Wales, is portrayed in the semi-autobiographical novel *O Law i Law* by T. Rowland Hughes.[38] The widowed mother, having acquired a mangle in this way, was able to support her young family by mangling blankets and sheets for 1½d. each, and tablecloths and other similar items for one penny each. Informants from the slate-quarrying villages of Bethesda (Caernarfonshire) and Blaenau Ffestiniog (Merioneth) recalled that this service was provided by mangle-owners at the beginning of the twentieth century. Informants from agricultural areas also stressed that dry-mangling large items reduced the work of ironing them. Within this community, mangles were regarded as valuable pieces of equipment, and to be in possession of one raised the status of a family. Yet, the reluctance to buy a washing machine within this same community is an unexplained enigma.

Smoothing Irons

To trace the development of the flat iron in conjunction with the first self-heated box iron is made difficult due to the variation in terminology found in Welsh manuscripts. A seventeenth-century inventory refers to 'one case of smoothing irons' in the house occupied by Gabriel George, yeoman of Penmark (Glamorgan) in 1678.[39] However, smoothing steels and heaters, steel boxes and smoothing irons are listed in eighteenth-century Welsh wills and inventories. It is evident that both smoothing steel and steel box are synonymous with box iron, with 'heater' being the general term used for the piece of iron inserted into the box. On the other hand, it is not as evident that the term smoothing iron is synonymous with flat iron. Here, the exact identification of the following items, namely, '2 iron heaters, 6 smoothing irons', listed as part of the kitchen goods and chattels at Derwydd in Carmarthenshire (1794), is not clear.[40] On the other hand, a record of the equipment provided for the laundry at Henblas, Anglesey (1730), namely '2 Box irons and 8 Flat irons'[41] points to the fact that both types of irons were in use concurrently in the early decades of the eighteenth century.

At this period, it seems that the ironing of all garments would have been done on an ordinary table covered with a blanket, as is suggested in the will of one Evan Bowen of Abergwili, Carmarthenshire (1746). He bequeathed 'the smoothing steel and the heaters and the blanket belonging to the same' to Jane Richards, his servant maid.[42] References are found in nineteenth-century Welsh inventories to deal tables for ironing, and it has been recorded that ironing boards of different shapes to suit specific garments were available in Victorian times, but oral testimony proves that these sophisticated items were not used in ordinary Welsh houses at the beginning of the twentieth century. Informants from most parts of the country referred to ironing on the kitchen table, covered by an old blanket and a top cotton sheet. They also confirmed that the flat iron was in general use until after the Second World War, while the use of the box iron, at this date, was generally reserved for ironing delicate items such as starched collars and shirt fronts.

The flat irons varied in size and were numbered from 1 to 10, with the medium sizes being the most suitable for ironing ordinary garments. Usually, a pair, used alternately, were heated by direct heat from an open fire, and although the flat iron did not retain its heat for a long period, it seems to have proved more effective than the box iron. All informants stressed that a well-stoked fire with a clean, red glow was a requisite for heating the flat irons, placed on a fire-bar stand in front of the fire or rested directly on the fire. Peat used as fuel was superior to coal in this respect as it did not soil the iron to the same degree. An ingenious method of keeping the flat iron clean while heating, used by some informants, was to rest it in an iron cauldron over the fire. Heating the irons to the correct temperature was a difficult task, and the usual method of testing it, as practised by the experienced, was to hold the base near the cheek, or to spit on it. To reduce the risk of scorching a garment, however, it was safer to test on a rough bit of cloth. When ready for use, the 'flat' would be cleaned by rubbing the base either on a board sprinkled with bath brick or on a clean cinder from the fire, or with soap or candle. Finally it would be polished with a clean cloth. A protective shield to encase the flat iron was a later innovation but on the whole proved ineffective due to the loss of direct heat.

Mrs Afanwen Davies, Pont-rhyd-y-fen, demonstrating the cleaning of a flat iron with soap, 1980.

The box iron, although cleaner, was also quite difficult to use, and when in contact with wet garments, such as cold-starch items, the heat loss was rapid and a large number of heaters was required to complete the task of ironing some two dozen collars. The heater, a wedge-shaped piece of iron, was placed in the fire and allowed to become red-hot before being inserted into the hollow box by means of a pair of tongs or with an iron poker. If overheated, it would expand and thus would not fit inside the box. When worn, it was also ineffective. New heaters were made to order by the local blacksmith. Other methods of internal heating were developed with the introduction of the charcoal iron and the spirit iron. In practice, the former was reported to emit soot, and the latter proved to be highly inflammable.

Ironing was a time-consuming task, usually tackled as soon as possible after drying and mangling. Most housewives paid special attention to this craft of smoothing their well-washed garments. Visible creases, commonly described as *traed brain* (crow's feet) were frowned upon. Ironed in the same rotation as they were washed, with the white articles given prime attention, all garments were then placed carefully on a line or bar, usually fitted above the kitchen fireplace, where they were then left for a few days to air.

Goffering Irons and Stacks

Rows of delicate frills and lace, which were used as decoration on caps, aprons, nightgowns and underskirts, required special treatment with goffering stacks or goffering irons. In early Elizabethan times, the pleats of ruffs and bands were set by moistening them with a starch solution and folding them, while wet, over a wooden or bone poking-stick of the desired dimension. The poking-stick was the forerunner to the simple goffering iron, shaped like a small soldering iron or poker, with a rounded end and a long handle, usually ornamented. It was heated in the fire and wiped carefully, and then a section of the fabric would be wrapped around it and held until it retained the tubular shape. An improvement on this goffering iron was the box-gofferer or tally iron (a corruption of Italian iron). Made in various metals, they were in general use in the eighteenth century. The heated bar was now inserted into a tubular case which was fixed horizontally on an iron stand, usually designed by the local blacksmith. A pair of bars would be used, in turn, to heat the case, and many examples were fitted with two cases of different dimension. The moist, starched fabric would be grasped in both hands and pressed over the tube to obtain a semi-circular scallop or flute effect. The large number of tally irons or box-gofferers donated to the Museum of Welsh Life provides eloquent testimony of their use throughout Wales in the nineteenth century. However, very few informants were able to recall their use at the turn of the twentieth century. The tubular stands remain as ornaments in many homes today.

Quilling or quicking lace-bands or trimming to produce a finer or closer effect was carried out on another device known as a goffering stack. Dating from the early eighteenth century, a goffering stack comprised a wooden frame about thirteen inches in height. The two upright pieces were fixed into a wooden base and were grooved to hold a stack of quills some six inches long. Continuing with the Elizabethan tradition of cold crimping, the damp, starched length of lace was wound around the quills and clamped down tightly, with pressure applied by the adjustable top bar, secured with wedges. The stack was then placed in front of the fire and the trimming removed when dry. These goffering stacks were used widely throughout Wales in the nineteenth century and some fine examples have been donated to the Museum of Welsh Life. One informant from the Llŷn Peninsula (Caernarfonshire) was able to recall that, as a child, she observed one lady using a goffering stack in the village of Bryncroes.

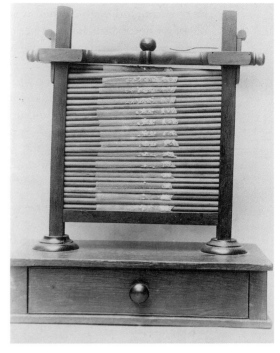

A goffering stack (approximately 38 cm high by 29 cm wide).

Crimping Boards and Rollers

To form minute crimping or rucking a crimping board and roller was also available from the early eighteenth century. It consisted simply of a grooved board and a correspondingly grooved roller. The damp starched fabric was laid on the board and a crimping effect was obtained by pressing the roller to and fro over the fabric. When used for gathering or rucking, the pleats were subsequently stitched at the top. A further development of this device was the crimping machine. Two fluted, hollow metal rollers were fitted on a frame, similar in form to a miniature mangle and turned by a handle. The fabric was inserted 'mangle fashion' between the rollers. Hot irons were inserted into the rollers at the free end, and thus the heated rollers accelerated the process of crimping. These irons were particularly popular with dressmakers during the nineteenth century and, again, the large number donated to the Museum of Welsh Life from different districts confirms their wide distribution and use in Wales.

THE WASHERWOMAN

It is not difficult to realize the volume of hard work involved in the laundering processes executed in the home. To cope with this enormous task together with other household commitments of baking, cleaning, churning and so on, it is not surprising to find that a high percentage of ordinary housewives were forced to employ casual labour. Thus the role of the washerwoman is prominent in the history of laundering in Wales. In contrast to the resident laundry maid, who, like the nanny, was a full-time employee of the richest families only, the *golchwraig* or *golchyddes* (washerwoman) has been prominent in all types of Welsh households. The Laws of Hywel Dda stipulate that an abbot be given the service of a *golchyddes* from his own race. Household account books of landed gentry record the regular employment of a washerwoman on a daily basis in the eighteenth century. For the period 1763–83 inclusive, regular entries for paying 'one washerwoman 1 day washing 4d.' or 'Pegi Frwd 3 days at 3d. for washing' are found in both the Edwinsford and Noyadd account books.[43] Similar evidence is found in the accounts kept by Elizabeth Martin for a yeoman's household in Glamorgan for the years 1763–5.[44]

The service provided by the washerwoman in Wales throughout the nineteenth century can be traced in documentary sources which, in turn, are confirmed by oral testimony. Authors of autobiographies, giving reminiscent accounts of their childhood years, occasionally refer to the role of the washerwoman in the local community. Elizabeth Williams, writing of her family in Anglesey and Caernarfonshire in the early twentieth century, notes that her mother regularly employed one Marged Jones for one whole day per week throughout the year to do the washing, to clean the house and complete the ironing, if drying conditions permitted, before returning home after supper. Her reward was one shilling plus her meal during the day. The same author refers to the second category of washerwoman who 'took in' washing, and coped with the task within the boundaries of her own kitchen. Marged Ifans, reported to be living in a tiny cottage, would be forced to keep the back door open, be it summer or winter, to accommodate the wash-tub in the confined space of her kitchen. She would provide this service for her regular customers for ninepence per dozen garments, irrespective of size. By being able to cope with it within the walls of her own domain, however, she qualified for higher social status than Marged Jones who had to abandon her home for the day.[45]

Oral testimony proves, without doubt, that these two types of service continued to be offered throughout Wales well into the twentieth century. Both farming and industrial communities relied on the washerwoman to help them contend with the arduous task of washing for large families. In the agricultural areas, the sparsely populated regions, with their scattered farmhouses and small mansions, a household would demand the employ-ment of a visiting washerwoman for a whole day. Her reward in the early decades of the century would not exceed one shilling and sixpence a day, plus her meals; a bonus of a loaf of bread or a hunk of cheese would be given periodically. In the larger villages within the farming community however, there was a greater demand for the second type of washerwoman. It was she who provided a service for the menservants employed in the neighbourhood.

The families of professional men (such as doctors and the local clergy) and local businessmen were also ready to take advantage of this service. The washerwoman would be seen collecting and delivering their laundry in a large basket, often balanced on her head. The same pattern prevailed in the industrial towns and villages both in north and south Wales, with the professional and businessmen's households dependent on the washerwoman to relieve their wives of the heavy task.

This casual employment, on the other hand, was of great benefit to the washerwomen themselves. It provided them with a living or, at least, made it possible for them to augment the family income. These hard-working women, proud to offer such a valuable service, were usually widows, or wives of low-paid labourers or craftsmen, or indeed unmarried women who had spent their earlier years assisting their mothers at this task and had eventually taken it up as a vocation. Generally, they were diligent and dedicated workers who succeeded in turning this arduous task into a skilled craft, which in turn provided them with a source of income. A typical example of such a woman was one Jane Jones, the wife of a low-paid slate-quarry worker at Betws Garmon, Caernarfonshire. At the turn of the twentieth century, she managed to buy a house for her family, namely Tan-y-marian, Betws Garmon, for the sum of £100. She bought it with the income she earned by washing for the local clergy's household. Her niece, when an octogenarian, put on record how her aunt would collect and return a hamper full of linen and personal clothing from the vicarage every Friday evening. Coping with the washing and ironing for a household of six members, who included three resident maids, was no mean feat.[46]

Due to the volume of work at hand, these women were forced to undertake heavy work for six days in every week, but on Sundays most of them were known to be ardent church or chapel attenders. They are reported to be women of good character, highly respected in their own community, with many of them also serving as competent Sunday-school teachers. Another typical example was a woman born in the village of Trawsfynydd, in the heart of Merioneth, in 1892. Following in her mother's footsteps, Miss Annie Williams, Ffatri, dedicated her whole life to being a washerwoman until her death in 1966. A proud and independent person, she was a faithful member of the local church and was described by a fellow-villager as an honest, kind person and always ready to assist anyone in need. She earned her living by washing for some twenty-four customers in the village and neighbourhood. This example not only illustrates the enormous amount of work accomplished, but also points to the continuity of the service rendered, and the demand for it, at such a late date. A whole day at the beginning and end of every week would be spent walking considerable distances to collect and return the laundry to respective customers. The tasks fulfilled on the other days would include carrying the required supply of water, heating it on the fire in the kitchen, washing in a wooden tub with the aid of soap, soda and a wooden plunger, bleaching, starching and drying. Her monetary reward, per item, was threepence each for the pillowcases, fourpence each for bolster-cases, sixpence each for sheets, tablecloths and blankets, and twopence each for collars.[47]

The availability of professional washerwomen who relied on this source of employment to support themselves and their families, and their demanding such a low remuneration for skilled service, undoubtedly delayed the general acceptance of mechanical laundering aids by the ordinary housewife. These factors, together with the prejudice regarding unsatisfactory performance of the new-fangled machines, prolonged the persistence of traditional methods. It was not until an electricity supply was brought into the rural areas of Wales in the late 1940s and early 1950s that the traditional laundering aids eventually became obsolete.

NOTES

[1] *The Odyssey of Homer*, translated by Richard Lattimore (USA, 1965–7), book vi, p.104.

[2] Joan Liversidge, *Britain in the Roman Empire* (London, 1968), p.121.

[3] Ibid., p.180.

[4] Edward H. Pinto, *Treens and Other Wooden Bygones* (London, 1969), pp.148–9.

[5] *Chirk Castle Accounts, 1666–1753*, edited by W. M. Myddleton (Manchester, 1931), p.182.

[6] Christine Walkley and Vanda Foster, *Crinolines and Crimping Irons* (London, 1978), p.51.

[7] National Library of Wales (hereafter NLW) MS Edwinsford 11.

[8] NLW MS Lucas 4290.

[9] *The Household Papers of Henry Percy, Ninth Earl of Northumberland, 1564–1632*, edited by G. R. Bathe (London, 1962), p.37.

[10] Ibid., p.124.

[11] G. Nesta Evans, *Social Life in Mid-Eighteenth Century Anglesey* (Cardiff, 1936), p.38.

[12] NLW MS Edwinsford 11.

[13] 'Llysnewydd Inventory', quoted by F. Breudeth in *Carmarthenshire Historian*, 4 (1967), 79.

[14] Henry John Randall, *Bridgend, The Story of a Market Town* (Newport, 1955), p.17.

[15] NLW MS Edwinsford 11.

[16] *Chirk Castle Accounts, 1605–1666*, edited by W. M. Myddleton (St Albans, 1908), p.126.

[17] NLW MS Peniarth 513D.

[18] *A History of Technology*, edited by C. Singer, E. J. Holmyard, A. R. Hall and Trevor I. Williams (Oxford, 1958), vol. V, p.834.

[19] Museum of Welsh Life (hereafter MWL) MS 2564: Notes on the history of the soap and candle factory, Llwynypia, Rhondda. Donor: Canon Cyril A. Davies.

20 MWL MS 2055: Grocer's account book owned by the grandparents of the donor, Mary Owen.

21 MWL MS 1510/7: Mary Winifred Jones, Cwm-main, Y Bala.

22 *Llyfr Coginio a Chadw Tŷ* (Wrexham, ?1850), p.312.

23 Pinto, *Treen and Other Wooden Bygones*, p.154.

24 Gwent Record Office MS D43.4157.

25 Francis Jones, 'Cadets of Golden Grove', *Transactions of the Honourable Society of Cymmrodorion* (1971), part 2, 265.

26 T. H. Parry-Williams, *Llawysgrifau Richard Morris* (Caerdydd, 1931), p.176.

27 *Facsimile of the Chirk Codex of Welsh Laws*, edited by J. Gwenogvryn Evans (Llanbedrog, 1909), p.28.

28 Parry-Williams, *Llawysgrifau Richard Morris*, p.176.

29 Pinto, *Treens and Other Wooden Bygones*, p.149.

30 Ibid., p.149.

31 Ibid., p.155.

32 Mary Norwak, *Kitchen Antiques* (New York, 1975) p.53.

33 Ibid., pp.57–8.

34 Pinto, *Treens and Other Wooden Bygones*, p. 152.

35 'Llysnewydd Inventory', p.79. See p.25 above.

36 Francis Jones, 'The Vaughans of Golden Grove', *Transactions of the Honourable Society of Cymmrodorion* (1963), part 1, 205.

37 NLW MS Edwinsford 11.

38 T. Rowland Hughes, *O Law i Law* (Llundain, 1944), pp.24–6.

39 Moelwyn I. Williams, 'Glamorgan houses and their interiors in the seventeenth and eighteenth centuries', *Glamorgan Historian*, 10 (1974), 166.

40 Francis Jones, 'Cadets of Golden Grove II', *Transactions of the Honourable Society of Cymmrodorion* (1972–5), part 2, 152.

41 Evans, *Social Life in Mid-Eighteenth Century Anglesey*, p.38.

42 Evan Bowen of Abergwily (1746), Will at NLW.

43 NLW MSS Edwinsford 11, Lucas 4290.

44 Randall, *Bridgend, The Story of a Market Town*, p.56.

45 Elizabeth Williams, *Siaced Fraith* (Llanrwst, 1952), pp.70–3.

46 MWL MS 2863/5–7: E. Hughes, Caernarfon.

47 MWL MS 2863/4: Life story of Annie Roberts Williams, Ffatri, written by Gwenda Evans, Trawsfynydd.

Sucan *and* Llymru:
Dietary Oatmeal in Nineteenth-century Wales

In common with most hilly regions in Britain, oats have long been the staple crop grown in the upland farming districts of Wales. Wales has often been described as a land of mountains or a land of hills and, while this is in some ways an accurate description, to the geographer the country falls into three divisions, namely lowlands, moorlands and mountains. The moorland areas, that is generally the land between 600 and 2,000 ft (180–610 m.) are extensive and form the largest portion of the country. Generally, the soils are heavy and cold, and moisture rather than sunshine and warmth is the outstanding feature of the climate, thus making farming in these areas predominantly pastoral. A characteristic view from these moorlands is that of a sea of hilltops, stretching as far as the eye can see, and between the hills deep V-shaped valleys with cultivated fields on their floors. For geographic and economic reasons the members of the farming community were obliged to exist almost exclusively on the produce of the farm. Many of these farms were of extensive acreage, but a large part of the land was usually rough grazing, a third was pasture and hay, and only the small remainder was arable, on which oats were grown.[1]

On interviewing informants concerning their daily menu and food patterns during the last decades of the nineteenth century and early decades of the twentieth century, it soon becomes evident that the home-grown crop of oats was of considerable value to every farmer, and that oatmeal was one of the basic ingredients used in many of the dishes consumed regularly by his family. Having been harvested and thrashed by the farmer, the cereal was taken to the local mill to be dried carefully in the kiln and then ground to the required degree of fineness. Subsequently, it was sifted at the mill to rid it of any husks and gross meal so that the *cynos* (that is, the annual supply of oatmeal for human consumption) was as pure as possible and was ready to be carried home and stored carefully in special oak chests. Thomas Pennant, writing in

1773, refers to these particular chests. When describing the hospitable reception given him by one Evan Lloyd of Cwm Bychan, a landowner near Harlech in Merioneth, he writes:

> He welcomed us with ale and potent beer to wash down *coch yr wden* or hung goat and the cheese compounded of the milk of cow and sheep . . . The mansion is a true specimen of an ancient seat of a gentleman of Wales. The furniture *rude*, the most remarkable are the *cistiau 'styffylog* (or the oatmeal chests) which held the essential part of the provision.[2]

These chests were always kept in a warm, dry room, usually in the bedroom above the kitchen. It was imperative that the oatmeal was packed tightly into the chest to keep it dry and free of air, thus preventing it from becoming sour. Bringing home the oatmeal from the mill was a very special occasion in every household, when members of the family would wear clean, white stockings in order to stamp and tread the meal as it was put into the chest. Men, women and children would take their turn to stamp on it to ensure that it was packed really tightly. Stored in this way, the meal would keep fresh and free of mites for twelve months or more.

Oatmeal and its by-product *blawd llymru* (flummery meal) or *blawd sucan* (sucan meal), were the basic ingredients of the semi-liquid dishes such as *uwd*, *griwel*, *llymru*, *sucan*, *bwdram* – dishes which were served regularly within the farming community of Wales at the beginning of the twentieth century. While processing the fine oatmeal, the miller would extract from the oat-grain its inner husks, to which adhered some of the finest nutritive substance of the meal. On sifting the ground oatmeal through large fine sieves at the mill, these inner husks would remain in the sieve, and would subsequently be ground finely to give the farmer the valuable meal known as *blawd llymru* or *blawd/bwyd sucan*. When available, this meal was used in preference to the more commonly used oatmeal when preparing the sour-grain soup known as *llymru*, *sucan* or *uwd* in different areas of Wales. During the course of my field-work study, I have found that this one sour-grain soup is invariably known as *llymru* in the counties of Anglesey, Caernarfonshire, Denbighshire, Merioneth, Montgomery and north Cardiganshire. In the village of Llangwyryfon, a few miles south of the coastal town of Aberystwyth, *llymru* and *sucan* are used indiscriminately for the same dish, suggesting that the change from one term to the other occurs roughly in this area. The term *sucan* is used in the remaining areas of Cardiganshire and again throughout the counties of Carmarthenshire and Breconshire. Further west in north Pembrokeshire the same dish is known as *uwd* or *uwd sucan* and, lastly, in Glamorgan it is known as *uwd sucan* or *uwd sugaethan*. Of course these divisions are fairly broad and it would not be too difficult to find exceptions, but the delineation of these areas is sufficiently accurate for the purpose of this discussion.

A glimpse of this variation in terminology is seen in one or two written sources. Lewis Morris, one of the learned Morris brothers from Anglesey, on visiting Radnorshire in 1760, had learned that *llymru* (one of his favourite dishes) was known by a different name in that county. He draws the attention of his brother Richard to this name in a letter, 'succan neu uwd y gelwir llymru yno a succan brithdwym yw bwdran (neu succan gwyn Môn yno)',[3] (there *llymru* is called *sucan* or *uwd* and *bwdran* (or Anglesey's *sucan gwyn*) is known as *sucan brithdwym*). The Walters English–Welsh Dictionary gives 'flummery' the Welsh alternatives of *llymru, llymruwd, sucan, uwd sugaethan, brwchan* and *mwdran*.[4] (*Brwchan, mwdran, bwdran* and *sucan gwyn* are names given to a dish which is basically similar to *llymru* and its counterparts but of a thinner consistency.)

Commenting on the evidence collected for the *Report of the Royal Commission on Land in Wales and Monmouthshire* (1896), the editors of the *Welsh People* state that semi-liquid dishes such as 'porridge or stirabout, called in Welsh *uwd* has probably in some form or other been an important part of the daily fare of the Welsh peasantry from time immemorial'.[5] The noun *llymru* is included in the well-known *Dictionarium Duplex*[6] and is given the Latin equivalent *puls* (a porridge) which, in turn, is defined in the Latin–Welsh section as 'rhyw fwyd a arferei'r *hen* bobl yn lle bara' (some food which the old people ate instead of bread). The adjective *hen* (old) is significant here in that it implies that eating *llymru* was at least as old as the oldest people living in the period around 1632. (*Puls frumentacea* is given the Welsh equivalents of *llymru, uwd sugaethan, llymruwd, mwdran*.)

References to food in the renowned Morris Letters are numerous. Writing in the mid-eighteenth century, the three brothers Lewis, William and Richard Morris, born of farming stock in Anglesey, but at that date earning their living as civil servants, provide a link between the food of the gentry and that of the poor, and show that they ate both. Having been brought up on semi-liquid dishes as children, they continued, partly from ill-health, but partly from choice, to enjoy them throughout their lives. *Llymru, bwdran, uwd* and *sucan* are specifically mentioned; for example, Lewis wrote to his brother William from London in 1757 longing for some of his favourite dishes:

Ni cheir yma ddim bwdran llygadog, na diod fain chwibsur . . . nag uwd ag ymenyn o dan yr ordd, na llymru a llaeth gafr unlliw.[7]

[Here, one does not get bubbly *bwdran* or small sharp beer, or porridge with butter straight from the churn . . . or flummery with goat's milk.]

William writing from Anglesey to Lewis in 1760 states:

Dyma fi er's pythewnos neu well yn ffaeliaw bwyta rhag rydded yw'r deintws . . . rhaid croesawu bwyd llwy, ysef uwd a llymru, succan gwyn, pottes sew, a phosel.[8]

[Here I have been for a fortnight or more unable to eat because of loose teeth – one must be satisfied with liquid foods such as porridge and flummery, white gruel, broth, pottage and possel.]

Travellers' observations on their visits to Wales in the early nineteenth century include occasional comments on the daily fare in different parts of the country. Benjamin Heath Malkin, having made two excursions through south Wales in 1803, states in his chapter on Glamorgan:

> The habits of living amoung the common people in Glamorgan are favourable to health . . . Their food is chiefly good wheaten bread with cheese, butter and milk in farmhouses. They use vegetables in large quantities . . . Flummery made with oatmeal is used frequently in the Vale, and almost daily in the mountains.[9]

Another visitor to Glamorgan in 1841 was Alfred Russel Wallace, the scientist, who stayed for more than a year on a farm near Neath. When writing of everyday food he gives a fairly detailed description of *sucan blawd* 'formed from the husks of oatmeal, roughly sifted out, soaked in water till it becomes sour, then strained and boiled when it forms a pale brown, sub-gelatinous mass, usually eaten with an abundance of new milk for supper'.[10]

From scattered written evidence, one deducts that this sour-grain soup was eaten quite regularly within the farming community in Wales until the end of the nineteenth century. The Land Commission Report of 1896 showed that *llymru* was still eaten in many parts of Wales as an alternative dish to the more commonly eaten *uwd* (porridge) and adds the remark that 'it was not such good food for a man who works as porridge'.[11]

On recollecting their childhood and young adult days, many Welsh authors who were born early in the twentieth century refer to *llymru* or *sucan* as a regular dish served in their homes at that time. Autobiographies and volumes of reminiscences published in the middle decades of the twentieth century serve as valuable sources of evidence of this nature.

I will now discuss in detail the preparation of sour-grain soup in different parts of the country. The study is based on evidence recorded orally in the field, which is now preserved in the tape archive of the Museum of Welsh Life. While interviewing elderly informants (between 70 and 80 years old) in the early 1970s, I found that collecting oral evidence regarding the preparing and serving of this particular dish in different parts of Wales proved a comparatively easy task. The majority of the informants interviewed had partaken of *llymru* or *sucan* quite regularly during the early years of their lives, and the female informants were able to give a fairly detailed account of how the dish was prepared. On carrying out this survey it soon became evident that local customs and practices observed while preparing and boiling this one dish played a key role, and were of equal importance to the basic ingredients to ensure perfect results. These factors show the relationship between food and local customs and traditions.

Llymru in the counties of north Wales was prepared by placing a large quantity of *blawd llymru* (known in some districts as *topyn*) or *blawd ceirch*

Mrs Catrin Jones, Bala, preparing flummery: Pouring oatmeal into an earthenware bowl.

The flummery mixture before it turns sour.

Straining all liquid from steeped oatmeal.

or a mixture of the two meals (according to availability) in a large earthenware pot. A certain quantity of tepid water and buttermilk was poured over the meal, and the liquid well stirred into the meal which then was allowed to stand for a certain period until the contents of the pot became sour. The period allowed varied from area to area according to the degree of sourness desired, which was primarily determined by local custom. Between three and four days was the average period quoted, but extremes of two and seven days were occasionally cited. Two informants in Anglesey referred to the use of a little yeast or a small piece of dough as a souring agent instead of the more commonly used buttermilk. Having attained a required degree of sourness, the mixture was then poured through a fine sieve into another wide-mouthed earthenware pot, the meal being squeezed between the hands to extract all the goodness from it. The meal itself was then used as animal fodder. This fine sieve was usually made from horsehair (*rhawn*), framed with a wide, round wooden band, and was generally known as *gogr rhawn*, or quite often it adopted the name of the food with which it was associated, namely *gogr llymru*. References to a simple, home-made wooden frame to hold the sieve above the pot were commonly made, which left both hands free to pour the mixture and to squeeze the meal. The frame was known as *rhastal*, *car* or *trol*.

When required, a certain quantity of this strained, sour mixture, known as *tewion llymru*, was poured into a *crochan* (cauldron) or *cetel* (cooking-pot) for boiling. The remainder of the mixture was kept in the earthenware pot, and subsequently all the starchy matter sank to the bottom leaving a clear liquid on top. To ensure that the *tewion* did not become too sour, this clear liquid would be poured off daily and would be replaced by an equal amount of cold water. While this supply lasted, a certain quantity of

The flummery liquid before boiling.

the *tewion* would be boiled on consecutive days and the contents of the pot well stirred before use. Boiling *llymru* was both a skilled and a strenuous task. The number of persons to be fed determined the quantity to be boiled and hence the size of the cooking-pot. On a large farm the quantity of *llymru* con-sumed was quite considerable! When bringing it to the boil, it had to be stirred continuously over a clear sharp fire. Generally, the cooking-pot would be suspended over an open fire. Many aspects of the boiling of *llymru* are closely linked with local customs.

Transferring the liquid into a saucepan.

Firstly, on my enquiring about the nature of the fire itself, many informants emphasized that a bright, sharp fire was required for boiling *llymru* – in contrast to the slow smouldering fire more suitable for boiling *uwd* (porridge). The fuel most commonly used was wood or peat. Local observations regarding the nature of the fire have been recorded in couplets which are readily quoted by informants in some districts today. In the village of Llanbryn-mair, Montgomeryshire, an informant related that

> tân llym o dan y llymru
> tân mall wna'r uwd yn well[12]

[a sharp fire beneath the *llymru*
a 'rotting' dead fire improves the porridge]

Another informant in Merioneth expressed the same contrast in a couplet:

> freshdân dan llymru
> mud-dân dan uwd[13]

[a sharp fire beneath *llymru*
a smouldering fire beneath porridge]

Secondly, the wooden stick used to stir the *llymru* played a key role in the whole operation, but its size and shape, and the name by which it was known, varied considerably from area to area. On asking for a detailed description of this wooden tool the most common reply given was 'something similar to a small paddle' or 'like a slender cricket bat' or 'a wooden spoon with a straight, flat bottom to it'. This stick would be carved from a straight piece of wood, most commonly ash, to give a fairly slender piece at the top but widening towards the bottom for stirring the boiling liquid thoroughly. The length of the stick would be determined by the depth of the pot. In Caernarfonshire this tool was known as *mopran* or *pren llymru*, as *rhwtffon* in Merioneth, and as *myndl* or *mwndwl* in Montgomeryshire and the extreme north of Cardiganshire. Owing to the intense heat and the length of time taken to boil a large cauldron full of *llymru*, a more ingenious type of stick was devised in some districts, which made it possible for the person to stand at a considerable distance away from the fire while stirring. The part placed inside the pot itself would be similar to the one I have already described, but it was then made to curve over the edge of the pot and extended over a length similar to that of a walking stick.[14] References to this particular kind of stick were made by informants in Caernarfonshire and Merioneth, where it was known as *mopran coes hir* and *wtffon hir* respectively.

The liquid forming a thin ribbon or 'tail' as it runs from the tip of the flummery stick.

Having brought the *llymru* to the boil it had to be stirred briskly until it thickened to a certain consistency. Methods of testing the consistency of the boiling mixture followed local patterns. The most general method practised was to hold the *llymru*-covered stick a few inches above the pot at short, regular intervals and observe the consistency of the mixture as it ran off the tip of the stick back into the pot. Informants in parts of Caernarfonshire (for example, the Llŷn Peninsula) stressed that it should form a long tail, sufficiently thick to cause it to break three times before reaching the bulk in the pot. Informants in parts of Merioneth and Montgomery would define the desired tail as similar in size to a rat's tail ('cynffon fel cynffon llygoden'),[15] and many other informants in the same county would describe it vaguely as a thin tail, but stressing that it should not break as it ran back into the pot. Other informants, for example in Caernarfonshire and north Cardiganshire, would simply state that it should be boiled until it became as thick as jelly, observing no tail! These local customs determined the final consistency of the dish.

Methods of serving and eating *llymru* followed a fairly general pattern throughout the counties of north Wales. The pot was placed on a special stand at the centre of the table, the stand being a flat, crude piece of wood known as *pren crochon*, *styllen*, *planc* or *car pren*. Each person would have a wooden bowl or earthenware basin and a wooden spoon; they would pour some cold, fresh or skimmed milk into their bowl and then with their own spoon would help themselves to some warm *llymru* and place it carefully into the milk. In Merioneth, informants related that black treacle melted in warm water would be used as a substitute for milk when it was in short supply during the winter months. It was served for supper regularly during the summer months and occasionally as an alternative to *uwd* during the winter months. Local tradition cited that *llymru* should be swallowed without chewing it. Informants frequently stressed this point by quoting the following phrase in English – 'slip go down, never come up',[16] or 'slick go down, never come up'.[17]

Pouring the flummery into a bowl.

The flummery, when set.

Another dish, closely linked with *llymru* but of a thinner consistency, was served in the counties of north Wales. Pouring a small quantity of *tewion llymru* (that is, the original strained sour mixture) into a saucepan, a certain amount of water was then added to it so that, when boiled, it attained a thin consistency similar to that of custard. This particular dish known as *sucan gwyn*, or *brwchan* in the counties of Caernarfonshire and Merioneth, and *mwdran* in Montgomeryshire, would be served occasionally for supper in these three counties. Poured into individual bowls, small pieces of bread, sugar or black treacle and sometimes ginger would be added, to taste. Renowned for its medicinal qualities, it was also regarded to be the most suitable dish to give a mother after she had given birth to a child.

Turning to *sucan* and *uwd*, the sour-grain soups characteristic of the counties of south and west Wales, the preparation of these dishes followed a pattern basically similar to that already described for *llymru*, but local customs once more played a key role.

Invariably using *blawd sucan* as the basic ingredient, oral evidence testifies that it was steeped in *cold water* (a further souring-agent was not quoted) and this mixture was allowed to stand for *one* night only. It was *not* allowed to become sour; only on interviewing informants in north Cardiganshire, have I found sporadic references to allowing it to steep for two nights until it acquired a slight acidity. On the other hand T. Rees states that *uwd sucan* was allowed to steep for a few days before straining and boiling.[18] The brief description given by Alfred Russel Wallace of the method practised in the Neath district also states that husks of oatmeal were 'soaked in water till it became sour'.[19] Yet, oral evidence collected widely throughout the counties of south and west Wales proves that *sucan* or *uwd sucan* had ceased to be strictly a sour-grain soup in these counties by the early decades of the twentieth century.

Straining the mixture followed a pattern identical to that already described for *llymru*, the fine hair-sieve being known as *basarn* in Pembrokeshire and as *gwagar rhawn* or *gwagar sucan* in other counties. Stirring the mixture continuously while bringing it to the boil was again noted as an important but arduous task, many informants stressing that it would be stirred constantly and in the same direction the whole time. The wooden stick used for stirring the mixture was described as being a short one, and was generally known as *pren sucan* or *pren uwd* (although the term *myndl* infiltrated into parts of north Cardiganshire). Methods of testing the consistency of the mixture as it thickened were observed, and in some instances were very similar to those quoted for *llymru*. Holding the *sucan*-covered stick above the pot, the desired thickness of the tail varied from being as thick as a cat's tail (*cwt cath*) to a vaguely described 'thin tail'. One informant in north Cardiganshire related that the mixture should be boiled until it spluttered (*ffrwtian*) and quoted the first line of a folk song, popular in that area when the informant was a young girl – 'Ma'r sucan yn ffrwtian, bois'[20] (The sucan is spluttering, boys). The spluttering noise implied that it had thickened and was ready to eat. Again some more general observations were given, that *sucan* should be boiled until it became 'as thick as jelly'.

This particular dish, *sucan* or *uwd*, was closely associated with the hay harvest in north Pembrokeshire, in parts of south and mid Cardiganshire, and in Carmarthenshire during the period when the farmers helped one another and a large number of helpers had to be fed. At this time *sucan* or *uwd* would be prepared in large quantities and carried out to the hayfield where it would be served as a meal for the workers at midday. Boiled in a large cauldron to the required consistency, it would then be poured into large tin pans which had previously been rinsed with cold water. Before carrying it out to the field, particular attention was paid to the surface of the *sucan* or *uwd* after it had set. Tradition has it that a smooth, even surface, free from cracks and with a slight sheen on it was a woman's pride and joy! It proved her skill in boiling the mixture to the desired consistency. Most informants in these three counties noted the significance of this even surface and many added the following local saying – that a cracked surface forecast that the maid who was responsible for boiling it was destined to marry an ugly fellow.[21] Most informants related that a young girl would boil a second pot full of *sucan* rather than take one with a cracked surface out to the field and face the mockery. Every woman took pride in presenting a well-set, even-surfaced pan full of *sucan* at all times.

Another local observation, noted frequently by informants in these counties, is that a perfectly boiled *sucan*, when cool and served with a spoon should cut 'as clean as liver' ('torri fel afu').[22] A large spoonful of *sucan* or *uwd* in a bowl full of cold milk, or sometimes served to the menfolk in home-brewed beer, proved very refreshing on a hot summer's day, but opinions differed as to its nutritional value.

Sucan, defined more clearly as *sucan hilo* in parts of north Cardiganshire, and as *sucan berw* in parts of Breconshire, was not particularly associated with the hay harvest in these parts of the country, although one informant did recollect carrying it out to the workers while they were cutting peat on the moorland. More commonly, however, it was served for supper during the summer months. The pot would be placed on a wooden or straw-plaited stand – known as *torch wellt*, or *torch ffwrn* – at the centre of the table, and again it would be served in cold milk.

Oral evidence regarding *uwd sucan* in Glamorgan today, as far as I can prove, is almost non-existent, and references to it in manuscripts are very sparse indeed. Cadrawd (T. C. Evans of Llangynwyd) a well-known antiquary in Glamorgan at the end of the nineteenth century and early twentieth century defines it as 'a dish made of the husks from the oats'.[23] In the same manuscript he defines *uwd sugaethan* as a dish 'made of oatmeal after having stood in water until it got sour'. On interviewing the most elderly Welsh-speaking informants in parts of Glamorgan, I have found their evidence to be very vague and incomplete; not one of them has referred to it as a sour dish, but they describe it generally as ordinary oatmeal porridge taken with cold milk.

Again, in the counties of south and west Wales, we find a counterpart to the *sucan gwyn* of north Wales. That is, a dish similar to *uwd* and *sucan* but of a thinner consistency. Water was added to the strained *sucan* mixture so that, when boiled, a consistency similar to that of custard was obtained. (Some informants related using a mixture of fresh oatmeal and cold water as a substitute for the strained *sucan* mixture.) Invariably it would be poured over small pieces of bread in individual bowls, and sugar, butter and sometimes ginger were added according to taste. This dish was known as *bwdran* or *bwdram* in Pembrokeshire, Cardiganshire and Carmarthenshire, and as *sucan brithdwym* in Breconshire. Served as a warm dish, it provided a light meal, especially suitable for invalids suffering from a stomach ailment. Informants in these counties referred also to the general custom of giving it to a mother after she had given birth to a child; indeed in parts of Cardiganshire informants recalled the custom of giving it to young babies as a substitute for milk. In the coastal areas of Cardiganshire, a meal of *bwdram a sgadan* (*bwdram* and fresh herrings), when herrings were in season, was greeted as a welcome change from the more ordinary day-to-day fare. *Sucan brithdwym* was taken most frequently as a drink, and informants recalled carrying it out to the reapers in the cornfields.

On seeking informants' opinions as to the nutritional value of *llymru* and *sucan* they would modestly refer to them as health-giving foods, and describe them as being both refreshing and delectable. However, I feel that their true opinions were expressed in the local phrases and adages so often quoted by them. The phrase referring to *sucan* as 'sucan slic a bola slac' (slick *sucan* slacks the belly), or another describing it as 'cino can llath' (the hundred-yards dinner) both hint that those partaking of it experienced pangs of hunger shortly afterwards. Similar observations are recorded in the following couplet stating that *llymru* was eaten instead of food!

> Llymru lled amrwd
> i lenwi bol, yn lle bwyd
>
> [Rather rough *llymru*
> to fill the stomach, instead of food]

On the other hand, *llymru* was held in high esteem by the older generation for its medicinal attributes, especially in helping to relieve a person suffering from a kidney ailment. Informants in Anglesey and Montgomeryshire referred to the local custom of taking a bowlful of *llymru* as a delicacy to whet the appetite of an elderly sick friend when visiting them. Many other informants, generally throughout north Wales, recall that their parents had asked them to prepare a bowlful of *llymru* for them when frail and weak with age. *Bwdram* with ginger was also taken generally as an effective antidote to the common cold.

Many metaphorical phrases and local idioms used in everyday speech today refer to these traditional dishes, now extinct. Describing a person as being 'cyn llwyted â llymru' (as grey as *llymru*) implies that he is 'pale and weak'; and the phrases 'fel sucan un-nos' (like one-night *sucan*) or 'fel sucan crai' (like raw *sucan*) refer to a weak or tasteless drink. As a child I often heard my own mother describing thick gravy as being 'mor dew â sucan' (as thick as *sucan*), although she herself had never made or eaten it. I have naturally inherited the phrase from her and still use it, when relevant. 'Gwell sucan meddiant na gwin cardod' (*sucan* owned is better than charity wine) is a well-known Welsh proverb and 'bwyta llymru â mynawyd' (to eat *llymru* with a bradawl) is a phrase used to refer to the impossible.

It is generally assumed that rye and oats were, in the country of their origin, weeds among other cereals and that, afterwards, where favoured by soil and climate, for example, in the poor sandy soils of central Europe and in mountainous districts, they prospered better than the wheat or barley and became the main crop.[24] Professor Günther Wiegelmann is certain that oatmeal was primarily a famine food at a very early period, and that only gradually did it grow to be a generally accepted food. Furthermore, he stated that it first found acceptance in everyday foods and not as a festival food.[25] Wiegelmann classifies soups, porridges and similar one-dish meals as survival dishes in contrast to meat, sugar and other more expensive items that are not essential for the sustenance of life.[26] The sour-grain soup *llymru* or *sucan* may be classified quite confidently as being a survival dish among the agricultural community throughout Wales during the nineteenth century. With innovations and changes in the pattern of day-to-day living, however, one may deduce from oral evidence that its role gradually changed before it became totally extinct. In the case of *llymru* in the counties of north Wales its medicinal attributes outlived its day-to-day use and it became confined to the invalid-foods category. The preparation of *sucan* in the counties of south-west Wales, on the other hand, in the early decades of the twentieth century was confined to the hay harvest and thus it could be classified as a dish associated with one period in the agricultural community calendar, giving it the role of 'festival food'.

The growing availability of a greater variety of foods, particularly tinned foods, in shops during the early decades of the twentieth century enabled the farmer to be less dependent on the produce of his own farm. Consequently, he was able to specialize in the type of farming best suited to his particular farm. In most of Wales farmers turned to various kinds of animal farming, particularly dairy farming, causing a comparative decrease in the growing of cereal crops, including oats. The result of these major changes in social habits was the total extinction of oatmeal dishes within a fairly short period of time.

NOTES

[1] E. G. Bowen, *Wales: A Study in Geography and History* (Cardiff, 1941), p.131.

[2] Thomas Pennant, *Tours in Wales*, 2 (London, 1810), pp.278–9.

[3] *The Letters of Lewis, Richard, William and John Morris of Anglesey*, II, edited by John H. Davies (1909), p.242.

[4] Revd John Walters, *An English and Welsh Dictionary* (Denbigh, 1828), s.v.

[5] J. Rhŷs and David Brynmor-Jones, *The Welsh People* (London, 1900), p. 562.

[6] J. Davies, *Dictionarium Duplex* (1632).

[7] *The Letters of Lewis, Richard, William and John Morris of Anglesey*, I, edited by John H. Davies (1907), p.461.

[8] Ibid., II, p.264.

[9] Benjamin Heath Malkin, *Scenery, Antiquities and Biography of South Wales*, II (London, 1807), p.543.

[10] A. R. Wallace, *My Life: A Record of Events and Opinions* (1905), p.181. 'This dish with thin oatmeal cakes, home-made cheese, bacon and sometimes hung beef, with potatoes and greens and an abundance of good milk forms the usual diet of the Welsh peasantry.'

[11] Rhŷs and Brynmor-Jones, *The Welsh People*, p.563.

[12] Museum of Welsh Life (hereafter MWL) tape, no. 3457, Mary Davies, Pennant.

[13] MWL tape, no. 2848, Mrs Mary Evans, Rhyd-y-main, Dolgellau.

[14] MWL tape, no. 866, Owen Griffith, Rhoshirwaun. (One informant gave detailed measurements of 10 in. and 3 ft 6 in. respectively.)

[15] MWL tapes, nos. 2837, Kate Edwards, Cwm Prysor; and 2840, Cathrin Jones, Llanuwchllyn.

[16] MWL tape, no. 2852, Ann Elin Morris, Parc.

[17] MWL tape, no. 3828, Mary Ann Jones, Bwlchllan.

[18] T. Rees, 'Bwydydd Sir Benfro', *Y Geninen* (1898), p. 247.

[19] A. R. Wallace, *My Life*, p. 181.

[20] MWL tape, no. 3828, Mary Ann Jones.

[21] MWL tape, no. 2723, Elizabeth Thomas, Beulah, near Aberporth.

[22] MWL tape, no. 2493, Rachel Morgan, Trelech a'r Betws.

[23] MWL MS 1406, Thomas Moreton Williams, Llangedwyn.

[24] R. U. Sayce, 'Food Through the Ages', *The Montgomeryshire Collections*, 49 (1946), 275.

[25] Günther Wiegelmann, '*Alltags-und-Festspeisen: Wandel und Wartige Stellung* (Excerpts of the Introduction translated into English by Roger L. Welsh)', *Keystone Folklore Quarterly* (Winter 1971), 206.

[26] Ibid., p.194.

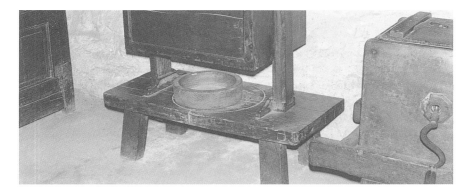

Cheese-making in Glamorgan

In pre-industrial Glamorgan most of the inhabitants were involved in agriculture, earning their living either by pastoral or arable farming or being occupied in related crafts and skills. The upland regions, or 'Y Blaenau', because of geographic conditions concentrated on the breeding of cattle, horses, sheep and goats and produced butter, cheese and wool. The low-lying regions of the Vale, 'Y Fro', with its richer, more fertile soil enabled farmers to practise 'mixed husbandry', that is the growing of crops as well as stock rearing and dairy farming.[1]

The production of butter and cheese played a key role in the economy of both regions well into the nineteenth century, and continued to be prominent in the upland regions until the early decades of the twentieth century. Primarily, butter and cheese were produced for home consumption but, as extant documents prove, surplus stock was sold to provide income. Indeed, these records provide a key to identifying the value of dairy products to the farmers and to proving their involvement with dairying skills.

As early as 1552–3, Thomas Phaer reported 'the great lading of butter and cheese along the Glamorgan coast'. Daniel Defoe, on his visit to Wales some 150 years later, recorded that south Glamorgan supplied Bristol with butter 'just as Suffolk does to the City of London'.[2] Port books provide a general record of the cargoes shipped from Cardiff to Bristol and the west of England in the early seventeenth century and, amongst other produce, butter and cheese are listed in detail. In 1600, for example, nearly twenty tons of butter and more than eighteen tons of cheese were exported to Bristol, the prices being distinctively higher than those obtainable in south Wales.[3]

Scholars studying the economic and social history of Glamorgan in the seventeenth and eighteenth centuries have also observed that the farmers and cottagers of Glamorgan found a ready market for their surplus dairy products in local shops, fairs and markets. Small farmers depended on gaining a quick monetary return for their produce. The inventory of one

Walter Hart (1696), in the parish of St Andrews, described as a blacksmith, farmer and shopkeeper, includes seven stones of cheese at 3s. per stone and a firkin of butter worth 16s.; another, Morgan David of Llantrisant, when he died in 1760, had 'butter in casks' valued at £19 and eighty-eight cheeses.[4] Other contemporary inventories are further proof of the production of butter and cheese in Glamorgan during the eighteenth century. It is not the aim of this paper, however, to consider the economic aspects of dairy products in Glamorgan at any one period, but to look in particular at the skills involved in the production of the types of cheese which were indigenous to Glamorgan.

GLAMORGAN CHEESE

Of Glamorgan cheese in the early nineteenth century, Walter Davies (Gwallter Mechain) writes:

> The principal object of the dairy in Glamorgan, as well as in all parts of South Wales, is butter; hence the great quantity of dry cheese (*cosyn cnap*) that are made therein. All the cheese in this county, especially of the Vale, has a shortness or brittleness not common elsewhere; some ascribe this quality to the abundance of white and red clover in the natural pastures.

He continues, giving a brief description of the method:

> To the morning's milk when it is brought in from the field, add the former evening's milk and both together warmed to the temperature of milk fresh from the cow; to this add the infusion of the vell or rennet, prepared the evening before. Break, collect, vat and press. These cheeses were made nearly, and often so thin as the Gloucesters, without any colouring. When the curds of one day is kept, to be broken and mixed with fresh curds of the following day, it is always kept covered with cold water.[5]

With the exception of this description of the traditional method of making cheese in the Vale recorded by Walter Davies, no other documentary evidence seems to have survived which gave details of the skills involved and knowledge of the materials and appliances used. One had to turn to the oral testimony and seek help from the older generation of inhabitants within the county who practised these skills in the late nineteenth century and early decades of the twentieth century. Unfortunately, while undertaking an oral history project, it was also difficult to locate such informants (in the 1970s) who could describe in any detail the method of making Glamorgan cheese. As was noted by one D. J. Jenkins, Great Frampton, near Cowbridge, in the *Report of the Royal Commission on Land in Wales and Monmouthshire* (1895): 'They have given up cheese-making very considerably on account of the difficulty of finding dairy maids'.[6] However, one lady, an octogenarian whose family originated from Pen-coed, near Bridgend, was interviewed at great length. She was well versed in the traditional skills of dairying in the area known as Border Vale in the county of Glamorgan, and the art of cheese-making as it was fully described by her has been recorded on tape. This information is now available in the Museum of Welsh Life's sound archive.[7]

To my knowledge, this informant was the third generation within her family who had been taught the skills of a dairymaid, skills that were transferred from mother to daughter, from generation to generation. It seems to have been the prerogative of the farmer's wife and daughters, in general, to be in sole charge of the dairy. As quoted by an old Norfolk farmer, 'they would be more likely than hired workers to attend to the essential cleanliness required there'.[8] My informant expounded on this all-important need for cleanliness from the outset. She emphasized that she was taught by her mother not only the method of making good-quality cheese, but also the importance of paying great attention to personal hygiene as well as practising good housekeeping regarding the care of all utensils and appliances used. In this context, her mother would reiterate constantly that 'their livelihood depended on the cheese' ('ein bywoliaeth yn dibynnu ar y caws'). Before beginning the daily tasks involved in cheese-making the informant would don a clean, long white apron and cap. On this family farm, the dairy was fitted with six slate settling troughs, of which one was reserved for cheese-making and the remaining five were used for butter-making. Cheese vats, cheese cloths and other accompanying appliances were placed on open wooden shelves close at hand and the cheese press took up a prominent position within the dairy itself.

CHEESE-MAKING APPLIANCES

Cheese Vats

Cheese vats (*cawstell, cawslesi* in Welsh-speaking parts of Glamorgan) were turned or coopered vessels made of hardwood, usually of elm, oak or sycamore. They were made in different sizes varying from 5½in. to 18in. in overall diameter and with an inside depth of 1½in. to 8in. – those over 6in. in depth were usually coopered.[9] The coopered vats were bound with iron bands. The base of most examples was pierced with draining holes and wooden lids or followers were custom-made to fit individual vats. The vats were filled evenly with fresh broken curd and placed in position beneath the weight of the cheese press. After use, great care was taken of the vats. They were washed, scalded in boiling water and scrubbed clean with fine sand. Finally, they were rinsed and allowed to dry thoroughly before storing.

Cheese Presses

The early cheese presses were worked by means of a drop weight. They could be constructed using one heavy stone, controlled by a rope and allowed to fall between two guide posts. The stone would be seated on a wooden platform, to which the cords were connected, or the stone itself could be fitted with an iron ring for suspension. Alternatively, the weight would be built up with a number of small stones placed in a large wooden box. This box would be

Wooden box-type cheese press, as used in Glamorgan in the nineteenth century.

hoisted by means of ropes within a vertical rectangular frame supported by a solid bench on four short legs. The ropes would be suspended from a windlass and ultimately controlled by a wooden cog-wheel fitted to the upright side-post. Having placed the vat in position on the circular groove on the bench base, the weighted box would be lowered gradually by adjusting the cog-wheel. These wooden box-type presses (known in Glamorgan as 'wrings') were made by local craftsmen, and some of them were highly polished; others had a more crude finish. Both single and double box-type presses were found in Glamorgan farmhouses; there are examples of both types in the Museum of Welsh Life's collection. To keep an even weight within each box was all important to provide a uniform pressure on the vats below. Two or three vats, carefully stacked one on top of the other, could be accommodated in a single press at any one time. The box-type presses were superseded by mass-produced cast-iron presses worked by means of screw pressure or lever pressure. It is known that these were in use in some farms in upper Glamorgan in the early decades of the twentieth century.

Cheese Cloths

Cheese cloth is a finely woven muslin which was used to hold the curds together in the vat. It was usually bought by the yard in a local store and cut to size as required. All informants stressed that these cloths, after use, had to be soaked in cold water, washed , boiled and hung out to dry in fresh air. To every dairy-maid, this was the daily task of paramount importance to ensure good results.

Vell or Rennet

Rennet is the agent used to curdle the milk when making cheese. In the medieval period, rennet was obtained from any young suckling animals which could best be spared for slaughter but, as more calves were bred, the calf supplanted other young animals as the provider of rennet for the dairy. The calf's vell or stomach-bag was taken out and the curd within it removed and cleaned. The vell was washed and salted and put in a pot with the cleaned curd inside it. The theory was that this meal would feed the vell and increase the flow of rennet. If the salted vell was kept for a long period, its own brine turned to rennet. Alternatively, fresh brine could be added later, which would also turn into rennet.[10] Walter Davies refers to the custom of using a calf's stomach-bag and the various stages of preparation carried out at home to produce rennet, but he adds that by the early nineteenth century it was prepared 'in most parts by the butchers: cleaned, but not washed with water, salted and dried upon a twig bent in the shape of a paper kite, and sold by them'[11] for, according to size, from one shilling to two shillings each. Part of this dried skin in proportion to the quantity of milk to be curdled was soaked in warm water overnight for use on the following morning.

Details of preparing and using a calf's stomach-bag was given by our informant. Her mother would purchase one, as needed, from the local butcher. Initially, it was boiled in salted water for a few minutes for further cleansing and then boiled in fresh milk until a slight aroma of cheese could be detected from the boiling liquid. It was then allowed to cool before adding a small quantity of the previous brew to activate the 'new' one, and to settle overnight before use.

METHOD OF CHEESE-MAKING IN THE BORDER VALE OF GLAMORGAN

The prime quality Glamorgan cheese (*cosyn llefrith*) was prepared during the summer months from the beginning of May until the end of August, using whole or full-cream milk only. The first key step was to process the milk immediately after it was drawn from the cow, while it was still at natural cow-temperature. Every morning and night, the 'new' milk was brought into the dairy and poured through a very fine sieve into a large earthenware pan. For every five gallons of new milk (usually the amount obtained from one milking session) a certain measure of the prepared rennet was added. It was difficult to ascertain the exact quantity used – a quarter bowlful was the given description – which could possibly be translated to mean a cupful. Experience and practice determined the required measure. The rennet had to be evenly dispersed and uniformly stirred into the milk with a purpose-made wooden stick reserved for this all-important purpose. It was then allowed to settle and curdle for some fifteen minutes. At this point, the very soft curd was cut gently with the wooden stick so that the whey (the liquid waste) began to separate from the freshly formed curd. The curd was given a further fifteen minutes to settle and at the end of this period, the whey would appear as a slightly green-coloured liquid. The next key step was to drain the whey from the curd while it was still slightly warm. If it became cold it would not separate from the curd and thus the curd would remain 'sloppy', which was not conducive to making good-quality cheese.

To break up the curd by hand was a skill taught to young girls at a very early age. Our informant recalled being asked to assist her mother at this task only, a task given to young females as an initiation to the skill of cheese-making. While it was still in the earthenware pan, and using the finger-tips only, the curd was broken up into small pieces 'resembling the size of hazelnuts', and the whey scooped away with a small wooden bowl. This process had to be executed very thoroughly until the curd appeared to be dry. It was then placed in a cheese vat or mould, which was lined with a fine cheese-cloth. At this stage, the vat would be supported by a wooden frame over an earthenware pan to allow for draining for some further twenty-four hours. Finally, the curd would be transferred to a clean vat, again lined with cloth. Finely rolled block-salt would be added to the curd as it was placed in the vat – a layer of curd and a thin layer of salt, alternately, until the vat was evenly filled. The cloth was then folded over the curd neatly, taking the four corners to the centre before placing the vat lid, or 'followers', in position.

In the first instance, a 2lb to 3lb weight would be placed on the lid and a delay of some further twelve hours would be allowed before placing the vat under the cheese press. Too heavy a pressure at this early delicate stage would rob and drain the cheese of its true quality and essence. Care for the cheese while it was under the press was another key stage in the whole process. The cloth was changed and the cheese turned within the vat daily until the cloth was found perfectly dry and could easily be removed from the cheese. This routine would take between three and seven days according to the size and weight of the cheese. It was of paramount importance to press the cheese perfectly dry to prevent it from turning sour or rancid at a later stage.

Increasing the pressure or weight daily, as required, was a major skill acquired by years of experience in cheese-making. Some three or four vats could be accommodated together under the one press as long as the freshly filled vat was given the lowest position thus enabling the whey to drain away freely without being in contact with the drier vats above.

STORAGE OF CHEESES

A freshly pressed cheese was very brittle and easily bruised with too much handling. On being removed from the press, it was initially allowed to settle for some two days on the vat lid in a suitable location in the dairy before being carried to the cheese room for further drying. In the larger farmhouses, a specific room was reserved for the storage of cheese, usually located on the first floor and aptly named *llofft y caws* (cheese loft). The windows would be fitted with wooden shutters and the aperture covered with fine gauze or mesh so that, when it was open, fresh air could circulate freely within the room, and all insects were kept away. My informant referred also to a cheese table which had been custom-made by a local carpenter on which cheeses would be stored within the cheese room. Its surface was constructed of ash boards to give a perfectly even surface and it was edged with a raised lip or border. It took pride of place in a central position in the room. The farmer's wife and daughters would concentrate on keeping the cheese room scrupulously clean at all times. Our informant referred to the local custom of inviting friends and relatives to 'inspect' the cheese room during a casual social visit to the farmhouse.

Full-cream cheeses matured very slowly, and as the rind formed it became pale yellow in colour. All cheeses were turned every morning and evening, but the rind of a good-quality cheese did not need to be rubbed dry with a cloth daily if it had been well drained during production. A 7lb cheese would take a week or ten days to harden and it would then be ready to sell. My informant recalled that most of the cheeses produced at her home in the early decades of the twentieth century were sold to regular customers who came to collect them from the farm. Occasionally, however, excess supplies would be taken to the weekly local market in Bridgend where there was always a ready sale for their farm-produced quality cheese.

On the other hand, a few cheeses would be reserved for family use during the winter months. While they were dried and stored over a long period, the rinds of the full-cream cheeses would become slightly tainted with mildew. This growth would be known locally as *crofen lwyti* (lit. a mildew rind) and would be scraped away lightly with a sharp knife. This mildew formation was a characteristic of a rich, well-produced cheese and, according to local tradition, a good-quality, mature, seven-month-old, full-cream Glamorgan cheese had some similarity to a good Stilton cheese.

OTHER VARIETIES

Sage Cheese

It was traditional in Britain in the late medieval period to use certain herbs to induce the curdling of milk. Herb coagulants were weaker than rennet and gave the cheese a bitter flavour. But herbs continued to be used in cheese-making in some parts of Britain well into the nineteenth century. For most people herb cheeses were regarded as an extra treat. Sage cheese could be described 'as green cheese within the narrower meaning of the term and if it was not green enough spinach juice was added to make it more bright to the sight, it also served to take off the bitterness of the sage'.[12]

In the early twentieth century, sage cheese was still made in the Border Vale of Glamorgan and was regarded as a summer delicacy. My informant recalled that her mother accepted specific orders for her 'speciality sage cheese' every year. She had assisted her mother in making it and was familiar with the whole process. Primarily, she noted that the vats used for pressing the sage cheese were shallower than the ones used for whole-milk or mixed cheeses, but usually were wider in diameter. Also, a sage-leaf motif would have been carved within the vats. The method of preparing the curd for a sage cheese followed that of the whole-milk cheese but, when breaking it, a finer texture was required so that the sage could readily permeate through it. Finely chopped sage leaves would be added to each layer of curd when filling the vat. Finally three whole sage leaves were placed carefully on a sheet of greaseproof paper and placed in a central position on the top layer of curd before putting the 'follower' in position, and the vat weighted down. After some twelve hours of light pressing, the greaseproof paper would be removed and the leaves allowed to remain in position while the curd was pressed. The pressing and the drying of the sage cheese again followed a similar pattern to that of the whole-milk cheese.

Mixed Cheese

A sub-standard or a compound cheese was also produced in the Border Vale using a mixture of full-cream and skimmed milk. My informant referred to it as *cosyn cymysg* (lit. a mixed cheese) or *cosyn dou laeth* (lit. a two-milk cheese). This type of cheese was usually made when cream was in great demand for butter-making. An evening's supply of milk would be allowed to settle overnight, skimmed on the following morning and the cream reserved for butter-making. This skimmed milk would be added to the morning's fresh milk and the whole quantity brought up to blood-heat by adding to it a small amount of hot water. My informant was also well versed in the method of making this type of cheese. Its production followed the same procedure as that for the whole-milk cheese, but it required a shorter period to harden in the cheese room before it was sold. Its consistency was not as rich and brittle as the prime-quality cheese, and it was generally classed as being 'tough and rubbery'. According to one eighteenth-century English author, 'such a cheese, if made and due age given it, will be as good a one as any man need to eat'.[13]

Ewes'-milk Cheese

Writing of Welsh cheeses in the mid-eighteenth century, William Ellis referred to the custom of milking sheep 'in the rich Vale of Glamorganshire. To this purpose some keep five or six score, which they always milk behind and get about a pint from each sheep.'[14] He adds that 'as their milk is of a very fat nature they mix it with skim milk of cows, when a little is heated they put in their rennet and make cheese that is of a short tartish nature'. Economic historians confirm that ewe-milking was practised quite extensively in Glamorgan throughout the eighteenth century, a task that was usually delegated to women. It was continued by some farmers until well into the nineteenth century. Records show that John Howell of Llantrisant, who died in 1692, had '17 milch sheep' whilst Robert Williams, yeoman, of Llancarfan had '30 milking ewes' worth £6 at the time of his death in 1709. In the parish of Monknash, on the sea coast, Robert Jenkin, yeoman, who died in 1687, had as many as '53 milk ewes valued at £17 13s. 4d.'[15]

The Revd John Evans, when travelling through south Wales in the first decade of the nineteenth century, referred to

> a kind of cheese made in some parts of the country of all sheep's milk, or a mixture of sheep and cows' milk, exceedingly rich and high flavoured; and when of a proper age, little if at all inferior to the boasted *Parmesan*. That made at Ewenny sells for one shilling per pound while that of the dairies about St Fagans brings 16 pence.[16]

Walter Davies writes of the attributes of ewes' milk for cheese-making in Glamorgan in the nineteenth century. He quotes the testimony of one Mr Gale: 'in the Vale, many depend more for cheese upon the ewe than the cow . . . the soil milk of the ewe is nearly equal in richness to the cream of the cow, and in cheese-making the milk of five ewes is considered equal to that of one cow'.[17] Davies elaborates on the period for milking ewes and on the method of making the cheese, quoting another witness, namely 'EW'. He states that ewes were milked for cheese from 1 May to 20 August, twice a day, and from then until September they were milked only once, and that in the morning; 'All breeders of cattle give the cows' milk to the calves during the whole or the greatest part of May, for this reason, in several instances, cheese of ewes' milk only is made.' The milk was heated to bring it up to 'cow-heat' and then they proceeded with the usual method as for making cow's-milk cheese. EW stipulates, however, that the curd of the ewes' milk 'should not be broken so small as that of the cows' milk'. He also adds that:

> the cheese most esteemed of the country people in general is that of ewes' and cows' milk together – the cows' milk always skimmed – this they called mixed cheese and is always sufficiently fat. Ewes' milk alone makes cheese that is exceedingly fat, but when made with proper care, its flavour is only agreeably rich.[18]

By the end of the nineteenth century, the use of ewes' milk for cheese-making in Glamorgan had been discontinued. Sheep milking was a highly skilled job but also a tedious one that was usually delegated to women. By this time, farmers found that dairymaids were reluctant to carry out this task and thus were finally forced to discontinue the production of cheese.[19] During the early 1970s I was unable to locate any informants who could describe the skill of milking ewes in any part of Glamorgan, nor to record any details of the method of making this particular cheese. It was referred to only as a product of the past. In the border county of Powys, however, the cheese of ewes' and cows' milk continued to be made well into the 1930s and I was fortunate in being able to locate women who were experienced in the skills of milking the ewes and of making the cheese. Using a mixture of skimmed cows' milk and the full-cream ewes' milk, the cheese, known as 'the golden cheese of Breconshire' was readily sold in local markets and further afield.[20]

Caerphilly Cheese

Turning to the hill farms of Glamorgan in the area already referred to as Blaenau Morgannwg, a report on the 'Agriculture of Glamorganshire' notes that in the nineteenth century the small farmer would support his family by rearing calves and sheep, and by producing mainly cheese and wool.[21] The ordinary farmer would keep between twelve and twenty Hereford cows. Throughout the winter months the available milk supply would be required for fattening the calves in time for selling in the pre-Easter markets. Tradition demanded that fresh veal was the favourite meat eaten on Easter Sunday in Glamorgan. As soon as the fat calves were disposed of, the cheese-making season began; according to the report, 'a considerable number of small farmers follow this class of farming, and though they cannot amass fortunes they are able to pay their way and make a living'. This class of farmers kept to the traditional pattern of farming which had been pursued from generation to generation. Cheese-making was an integral part of that tradition; as stated in the report it 'runs in an old groove'.

However, it proved difficult to find documentary evidence for cheese-making in Blaenau Morgannwg before the early nineteenth century. The *Welsh Almanack* for both 1699 (Thomas Jones) and 1726 (John Rhydderch) give lists of Welsh fairs and markets held annually in Caerphilly. The dates for seven fairs and three 'great' markets are given, when cattle and woollen goods were the main commodities on sale. By the nineteenth century, however, Samuel Lewis in his *Topographical Dictionary of Wales* (Vol. I, 1833) wrote of Caerphilly: 'At the numerously attended fairs cows, cattle and cheese were the principal articles exposed for sale.'

An account book for the retailing of cheese at Tŷ Vaughan Shop, Eglwysilan, near Pontypridd, records business with local customers for the period 1835–70. Customers are identified frequently by name and craft, for example: 'Rees Thomas, mason who purchased 4lb cheese for 2s. 8d. on 29 April 1836 and Thomas Edwards, shoemaker, 5lb cheese for 3s. 4d. on 29 November 1837.' David Moses, schoolmaster, John Harris, woodcutter, and William Lewis, labourer, were also purchasers of cheese during this period. Other customers are identified by name and address. The purchasing of cheese cloth by farmers such as William Rowland, Pontygwindy (6 yds of cheese cloth 3s. on 6 April 1852) and John Edmunds, Gwaingledr (4 yds cheese cloth 2s. on 4 September 1856) is further proof of local involvement with cheese-making at this period.[22]

It is now appropriate to discuss briefly the method of cheese-making on the hill dairy farms of Blaenau Morgannwg – the cheese that was given the generic label of 'Caerphilly cheese'.

Specific references to Caerphilly cheese are given in the *Report of the Royal Commission on Land in Wales and Monmouthshire* (1895).[23] One Richard Jones describes it as 'the most remunerative cheese of what I term the native cheese'. He continues:

> A very considerable number of farmers, particularly in mountain districts, make Caerphilly cheese. It has this special advantage that it is ready earlier than any cheese, it is ready for market in about a fortnight to a month from the time it is made and it usually realises about 6d. to 7d. per pound. [It] is about an inch and a half thick and you can make it as broad as you like, but is usually made about 15 in. broad and a good number less than that.

In his report on Caerphilly cheese, W. Little noted that

> the Welsh farmer's wife may not know much of cream separators or the most scientific methods of dairy manipulation, but she is cleanly and careful and she produces an article of diet to meet local wants which is appreciated in any form whether mild or matured.[24]

I have been able to record in great detail oral evidence from farmers' wives and daughters who were experienced in making cheese in the Caerphilly district. Two informants in particular provided a very full account of the whole process. Within living memory, these two farmwives proved to be the third generation within their respective families to have been taught the skill of cheese-making.[25] On comparing their method with that already given by the informant from the Border Vale, it soon became apparent that they followed the same key stages and their methods proved parallel even in many minor details. Basically, they were all producing a semi-soft cheese, using whole or full-cream milk while it was in 'cow-temperature', and to which a specific amount of curdling agent was added. This was the essence of the Glamorgan cheese or *cosyn llefrith* (lit. a fresh-milk cheese) as it was described by the informant from the Border Vale, and similarly with the cheese now described by the two informants as Caerphilly cheese. In the latter instance, both informants referred to adding commercially prepared rennet to the daily supply of milk, but the setting of the curd, and its breaking to the stipulated size of hazelnuts was again observed. The method for filling the cheese vats and the daily care for the cheeses while draining under pressure followed the same pattern. Both informants emphasized that precision pressing was the key to producing a good-quality cheese, thus corroborating the testimony of the informant from the Border Vale. Applying the required amount of pressure to drain the cheese thoroughly but without pressing it until it became 'as hard as a brick', required great skill and experience, and the final proof of a well-drained cheese was that it should 'have some play in it'.[26]

Drying the cheeses in the cheese room was similarly observed, turning each one twice daily until it was ready to sell. A 7lb cheese would be sold within some seven to ten days. If stored for a period of six to nine months, however, a good-quality cheese would mature by developing some blue veins throughout, similar to those found in Stilton-type cheese. It would also have a creamy fragrance. Both informants also referred to making small amounts of 'sage cheese' for home consumption or for specific orders only. 'Cuckoo cheese' was another speciality cheese, made by both families. Basically it was the same whole or full-cream cheese, but this name was given specifically to the first batch of cheese made in the spring each year. This coincided with the arrival of the cuckoo in the rural areas with its long-awaited call. The cuckoo cheese would be sold immediately after its removal from the press. It would *not* be allowed to dry for the regular period of seven to ten days. This 'first of the season' cheese was in great demand by customers and thus it gave the farmers a very prompt monetary return which was also very acceptable after the lean winter period.

Cheese was produced on these two hillside farms near Caerphilly until the early 1930s, and tradition has it that they were the last of the farming families to produce the genuine Caerphilly cheese.

CAERPHILLY CHEESE MARKET

By the mid-nineteenth century, references to holding a weekly cheese market on the Twyn in Caerphilly are numerous. The population explosion in the Cardiff area during this period (1,870 inhabitants in 1801 compared with 32,954 in 1861), together with the influx of coal-mining families to the industrial towns and villages of south-east Wales, gave rise to a great demand for the mild-flavoured cheese sold in Caerphilly market. It was reported in 1850 that miners were prepared to pay 7d. per pound for Caerphilly cheese rather than buy the cheaper American brand, the only other alternative available to them, at 3d. per pound.[27] In their estimation, Caerphilly cheese, with its relatively high salt content helped to replace their energy after working underground in a bath of perspiration.

To meet the demand for cheese, farmers would flock to the weekly market at Caerphilly, transporting their produce by horse and cart or by train. They travelled from as far afield as Chepstow in the east and Cowbridge in the west. Trade merchants from a wide area were also present. According to

The Market Hall, Caerphilly, built 1889. (With kind permission of Rumney District Council)

weekly market reports published in the local press, it is evident that the cheese market in Caerphilly grew to an all-time peak in the period from 1870 to 1895. The first cheese of the season, usually sold in April, fetched high prices. In the *Cardiff Times* for 12 April 1873 a report on the second day of the April Fair noted that the cheese market for the year had begun. The price of the cheese offered for sale was between 65 and 67 shillings per hundredweight (cwt.).[28] The same buoyant and brisk trade is reported in the same newspaper twenty years later. On Wednesday, 8 April 1893 in Caerphilly: 'The first lot of new cheeses for the season were pitched in the fair today, which met with ready sale at the following prices: first quality 66s., seconds 63s. and thirds 60s. per cwt.'[29] A typical report from 1895, pointing to brisk business at Caerphilly market on Thursday, 1 August, appeared in the *Western Mail* on the following day:

> Today has been no exception to the splendid average of attendances of
> dealers and others at our weekly cheese market. The supply was good and
> of excellent quality and the business done was testified practically by the
> fact that all was cleared at prices ranging from 53s. to 57s. per cwt.[30]

In addition to the weekly markets, specific cheese fairs were also held in the market hall during the months of April, July, August, October and November. An annual cheese show was also held in the same building in September. The sixth annual Caerphilly Cheese Show was held on Thursday, 26 September 1895, and the following report was published in the *Western Mail*. The attendance and exhibits were all that could be desired. The judges for cheese and butter were Messrs D. B. Jones, The Terrace, Rhymney, and G. Austin, Nelson.

Pitch of Cheese of not less than 2 cwt.:	1st £3. Miss Williams, Spring Meadow, Lisvane
Pitch of Cheese of not more than 1 cwt.:	1st Miss A. F. Lewis, Bedwas House, Bedwas
	2nd Mr T. Jones, Marshfield
Single Cheese:	1st Mr R. Thomas, Jnr, Llanedarne
	2nd Mr W. Jones, Marshfield[31]

The buoyant and lucrative cheese market with its steady trading for some twenty years demanded a custom-built building where business could be carried out more effectively. A new building was opened on 26 September 1889 and the official opening was recorded in great detail in the national daily paper on the following day. It was an occasion for great celebration for the whole town.

> On Thursday the town of Caerphilly was *en fête*, the occasion being the opening of the new market buildings erected by Mr Alderman David Lewis and of which Mr Phillips of Cardiff was architect and Mr Rawson of Cathays the contractor. At 10.00 a.m. Mr Councillor Henry Anthony presented to Mrs David Lewis, on behalf of his fellow citizens, a gold key, with which the lady opened the market to the many hundreds of visitors present. The hall, which measures 100 ft. by 33 ft. was very tastefully decorated by Mr Farnworth of Messrs Cross Bros. Caerphilly and inside was stored in all probability the largest quantity of cheese ever pitched in the town. The whole of the inhabitants celebrated the occasion by a general holiday and the streets were in the afternoon paraded by a procession of tradesmen's and farmers' vehicles. There were also athletic sports and numerous other amusements got up by the town committee, of which Mr Thomas Thomas was chairman, Mr John Gibbon, secretary, and Mr W. W. Williams, treasurer.[32]

During the last decade of the nineteenth century the practice of sampling or branding the cheese for quality was initiated at the market in Caerphilly and a local inhabitant, Edward Lewis, caretaker of the new Market Hall, was appointed as official cheese-tester. He would use a horn scoop or gouge to sample the cheeses which, if found to be of standard quality, would be marked by the official circular stamp, namely 'Caws Cymru, Caws Pur: Genuine Caerphilly Cheese' with a central logo depicting Caerphilly Castle .[33] It is of interest to note that the Welsh term 'Caws Cymru' (lit. cheese of Wales; 'Caws Pur', lit. pure cheese) verifies the name given to this local cheese by the Welsh-speaking inhabitants in the Caerphilly area and adjoining villages at the turn of the century.[34] To the trade merchants, no doubt, the cheese was synonymous with the market town of Caerphilly. In turn, the adopted English name of Caerphilly cheese was translated literally by Welsh-speaking immigrants and the original Welsh term was gradually lost.

The practice of branding the cheese for quality and authenticity continued into the twentieth century. A 'Welsh Farmer' wrote to the *Western Mail* in December 1901 to express great concern regarding the depleted supply of cheese produced for sale at the Caerphilly cheese market. He also referred to the demise of the practice of branding the cheese for quality.[35] Edward Lewis replied to this letter, refuting this accusation and adding: 'the practice of branding the pure article has never fallen into disuse as the many respectable Welsh farmers who regularly attend the market can testify'.[36] Mr Edward Lewis was a gentleman of great integrity, as testified in the obituary notice published shortly after his death in December 1909 at seventy-four years of age. Described as a 'highly respected citizen of Caerphilly', he had held many public offices in the town. He was one of the oldest members of Bethel Welsh Congregational Church where he served as a Sunday school teacher for over fifty years.[37]

There is no further evidence of the practice of branding cheese in Caerphilly market. However, it is evident that a sharp decline in the Caerphilly cheese trade occurred in the early twentieth century. A report published in the *Western Mail* following the market on Thursday, 20 September 1900 read: 'A fair attendance of farmers and dealers characterised the market today. The supply, through being somewhat limited, ran the prices up, the bulk selling at 63s. to 65s. per cwt.'[38] No further market reports for 1900, nor for the whole year of 1901, appeared. Moreover, a leading article, published

Mr Edward Lewis, caretaker of the Market Hall, Caerphilly, appointed official cheese-taster during the 1890s.

The official stamp used by Mr Edward Lewis.

in the *Western Mail* in December 1901, expounded on the steady decline of the local cheese trade. The author of the article, entitled 'Caerphilly Cheese, Decline of an Ancient Industry', gave many possible reasons for the downward trend in the trade.[39] Primarily, it was noted that the farmers who formerly 'had made it chiefly their business to manufacture real Caerphilly cheese now find it more profitable and less laborious to send their milk for sale in Cardiff'. The demand for the daily supply drained all the dairies in the surrounding districts within a convenient radius of the town, and upwards of 30,000 gallons of milk were delivered annually to Cardiff.

The production at Highbridge, Somerset, of a new cheese of similar quality to that of Caerphilly was another possible factor. It was reported in the article that supplies of Somerset and Dutch imitations were finding their way to the local Caerphilly markets and were 'sold so much cheaper to the unsuspecting retail customer that the home-made article is being pushed out of the market'. No doubt it was the introduction of 'foreign' cheeses to the local market that motivated the local producers to have all cheeses tested and branded for authenticity and quality.

The author of the *Western Mail* article touches on other issues but returns to the prime factor of an increasing demand for daily deliveries of fresh milk around Cardiff which offered a new source of income to the local farmers. He had interviewed the caretaker of Caerphilly market who had reported to him that 'not an ounce of cheese had been brought into the market that day'. He quotes Edward Lewis: 'Twas not ever thus and it is perfectly clear that the manufacture of Caerphilly cheese is rapidly on the wane.'

An editorial comment on this article on the same day highlights the 'crisis of the local cheese industry' and expresses regret that an old establishment industry was in danger of being discontinued. The editor wished to draw the attention of the Welsh Industries Association to the problem and proposed that they or the technical instruction committee of the Glamorgan County Council look into the matter and suggest means by which the industry might be re-established on a firm footing. But he also stated that it was a question that the farmers had to determine for themselves.

During interviews with the informants who were among the last producers of the genuine Caerphilly cheese, they recalled that the Caerphilly cheese market had finally closed *c.*1910, but that they had continued to produce cheese, finding a ready market for it with local grocers in the Caerphilly and Tongwynlais area until *c.*1928–30. They sold the cheese for 6d. to 7d. per pound, this being their only method of generating an income from their milk supply. They had opted against following the general trend of turning to selling milk. A local historian, writing on the decline of the cheese industry, recalls buying the genuine, locally produced cheese in a specific store in Market Street, Caerphilly, between the mid 1930s and 1940. Rees's Stores was deemed to be one of the last, perhaps *the* last, to sell locally made Caerphilly cheese. He makes the point that 'this was the product of local farms and was *not* factory made'.[40]

To conclude, it is evident that, during the early decades of the twentieth century, the hill farmers of Blaenau Morgannwg gradually took the option of meeting the demand for fresh milk and became vendors of 'the daily pint' rather than the producers of cheese. It was the establishment of the Milk Marketing Board in 1933, however, that finally caused the demise of this domestic craft. From that date, milk supplies were collected daily in metal churns from every farm and taken to the local 'milk factory' for processing and distribution.

The story of cheese-making in Wales continues. In 1983, dairy farmers were confronted with new regulations with the introduction of specific milk quotas for every farm. They were forced once again to look at alternative methods of generating income from their milk supplies. Now the wheel had completed a full circle and the overproduction of fresh milk, together with the European 'butter mountain', posed a major problem for dairy farmers all over the country, and many of the more enterprising farmers, especially in south-east Wales, reverted to traditional methods and looked at the possibility of making cheese. I was approached by many farmers requesting recipes for traditional Welsh cheese and was able to offer them, amongst others, the recipe for the semi-soft full-cream Caerphilly-type cheese. Today, 'Caws Cenarth', 'Caws Nantybwla' and 'Caws Teifi' are amongst the well-known delicacies produced on specific farms and are sold not only on local market stalls and in delicatessen stores in Wales but are also in great demand in the most prestigious stores in London. In this age of mass production it proves once again that 'small is beautiful' and there is a lucrative demand for genuine, traditional, farm-produced Welsh cheeses.

In 1999, Caerphilly County Borough Council asked the National Assembly to support its bid to receive regional registration to make Caerphilly cheese, following the launch of Castle Dairies' organic Caerphilly cheese, produced on the Pontygwindy Industrial Estatue using the traditional whole-milk method. Under the strict rules of the European licence, Caerphilly cheese would have to be made using only milk from dairy farms in the borough, causing uproar amongst cheese-makers in west Wales who had been making Caerphilly cheese according to the traditional recipe since the early 1980s. John Savage-Onstwedder of Tivy Cheese was quoted in the *Western Mail* as saying 'You can make Cheddar anywhere in the world and the same should apply to Caerphilly.'

Caws Cymru, Caws Pur
Genuine Caerphilly Cheese

NOTES

[1] Moelwyn I. Williams, 'The economic and social history of Glamorgan, 1660–1760' in *Glamorgan County History*, IV (1974), pp.321, 334.

[2] Glanmor Williams, 'The economic life of Glamorgan, 1536–1642' in *Glamorgan County History*, IV (1974), pp.64–5.

[3] William Rees, *Cardiff: A History of the City* (Cardiff, 1969), pp.123–4.

[4] Moelwyn I. Williams, 'The economic and social history of Glamorgan, 1660–1760', pp.349–51.

[5] Walter Davies, *General View of the Agriculture and Domestic Economy of South Wales*, II (1815), pp.229–31.

[6] *Report of the Royal Commission on Land in Wales and Monmouthshire*, I (1895), p.16.

[7] Museum of Welsh Life (hereafter MWL) tapes, nos. 3053–4, 3074, Miss Cissie Davies.

[8] Fussell, *The English Countrywoman*, AD 1500–1900 (London, 1953), pp.194–9.

[9] Edward H. Pinto, *Treens and Other Wooden Bygones* (London, 1969), pp.102–3.

[10] C. Anne Wilson, *Food and Drink in Britain* (London, 1973), p.158.

[11] Walter Davies, *General View of the Agriculture and Domestic Economy of South Wales*, p.226.

[12] William Ellis, *Country Housewife's Family Companion* (London, 1750), pp.335–6.

[13] C. Anne Wilson, *Food and Drink in Britain*, pp.161, 178–9.

[14] William Ellis, *Country Housewife's Family Companion*, p.34.

[15] Moelwyn I. Williams, 'The economic and social history of Glamorgan, 1660–1760', p.326.

[16] Revd John Evans, *Tours through South Wales* (1804), p.193.

[17] Walter Davies, *Country Housewife's Family Companion*, p.227.

[18] Ibid., pp.229–31.

[19] *Report of the Royal Commission on Land in Wales and Monmouthshire*, p.16.

[20] Margaret Price, *Hanes Plwyfi Crai Brycheiniog*, II (1965), p.171.

[21] W. Little, 'The Agriculture of Glamorganshire', *Journal of the Royal Agriculture Society of London*, 21 (London, 1885), 186–8.

[22] *Glamorgan Record Archives*, D/D Xhs 3/1: Tŷ Vaughan Shop, 1835–70 Business Records.

[23] *Report of the Royal Commission*, V, p.257.

[24] W. Little, 'The Agriculture of Glamorganshire', p.182.

[25] MWL tapes, nos. 2692–3, Mrs Arthur Roberts, Morgraig Cottage, Thornhill; MWL tapes, nos. 2684–5, Mrs Prichard, Cefncarnau Uchaf, Thornhill.

[26] MWL tape, no. 2692, Mrs Blanche Roberts.

[27] Ieuan Gwynedd Jones, 'Merthyr Tudful in 1850', *Glamorgan Historian*, 4 (1967), 36.

[28] *Cardiff Times*, 12 April 1873, p.7.

29 Ibid.

30 *Western Mail*, 2 August 1895, p.3; for further reports for 1900, see *Western Mail*, 6 April, 15, 29 June, 13, 20 July, 17, 31 August, 7, 14, 21, 28 September, all p.3.

31 *Western Mail*, 27 September 1895.

32 Ibid., 26 September 1889.

33 By courtesy of Edward Lewis's great-granddaughter, Mrs J. Morgan, and family, this stamp has been donated to the Museum of Welsh Life, as well as information regarding the custom of branding.

34 Ex info. Dr Ceinwen Thomas, 22 February 1984.

35 *Western Mail*, 13 December 1901, p.3.

36 Ibid., 8 December 1901, p.3.

37 *South Wales Daily News*, 10 December 1909.

38 *Western Mail*, 21 September 1900, p.3.

39 Ibid., 10 December 1901, p.3.

40 Glyndwr G. Jones, *Cronicl Caerffili*, No. 4.

Traditional Breads of Wales

They eat meat in abundance, but very little bread.

Traditional descriptions of early Welsh diet and economy are based to a large extent on statements made by that shrewd observer, Gerallt Gymro (Giraldus Cambrensis). When journeying through Wales with Archbishop Baldwin in 1188, he placed on record in *Description of Wales* his view of the Welsh character and his impressions of Welsh society. The economic basis of their society was the pasturing of flocks and herds. 'Most of their lands', he said, 'serves for grazing, little of it is used for tillage, still less for gardens and scarcely any for orchards.' He noted that most of the people lived on the produce of their herds, with milk, butter, cheese and oats being staple articles in their diet. He added, 'they eat meat in abundance, but very little bread'.[1]

However, his statement that the Welsh ate little bread, or did very little ploughing except in March and April for the sowing of oats, can be counterbalanced by other evidence which reveals the basic importance of bread and of tillage. Indeed, the detailed attention given to the ox and the ploughman in the Laws of Hywel Dda, for instance, emphasizes the importance of tillage even in pre-Norman times. Ffransis G. Payne in his book *Yr Aradr Gymreig* (The Welsh Plough) has supplied ample evidence of Welsh tillage and its social implications from the tenth to the fifteenth centuries.[2]

The Laws of Hywel Dda codified in the eleventh century provide sound evidence of the growing of wheat, barley and oats as main crops, and both wheatbread and oatbread are specified as part of the food-tithe paid to the king by bondmen and freemen alike. Included in a winter's food-tithe were 'sixty loaves of wheaten bread if wheat is grown . . . if not, let the bread be oaten'.[3] Archaeological excavations at Dinas Powys, Dinas Emrys and Pant-y-saer, Glamorgan have all produced hand-mills for grinding flour.[4] This evidence again shows the importance of cereal crops despite Gerallt's assertions to the contrary. It is reasonable to conclude that this early Welsh economy was based on mixed farming, more or less adapted to local conditions of soil, altitude and climate. This economy sufficed to provide the people with a subsistence diet based mainly on meat, dairy produce and oatbread. Gerallt Gymro described the Welsh as not being addicted to gluttony, but dedicating their whole day to work, and in the evening partaking of a moderate meal. Guests were welcome and a meal would be prepared according to the number and dignity of the persons assembled and the wealth of the family who entertained.

> The kitchen did not supply many dishes nor high seasoned incitements to eating: the home is not adorned with tables, cloths and napkins, they study nature more than splendour for which reason they place all the dishes together upon rush mats and on large platters, around which the guests sit in threes and not in pairs as in other countries. They also serve the food on large thin cakes, baked daily.[5]

Despite a more systematic approach to land cultivation following the Tudor enclosures, and with the growing of crops for home consumption established on a firmer footing, farming in Wales still remained predominantly pastoral. Meat was eaten regularly, and the bread was made of oats or rye.

Writing during the reign of Elizabeth I, the Pembrokeshire historian, George Owen of Henllys, described the diet of the poorest husbandman in his country thus: 'the common foode is beefe, mutton, pigge, goose, lambe, veale and kydd.'[6] He also notes that they persisted in growing oats, as did their fathers in previous centuries, on land suitable for producing wheat or rye; they preferred *yr hen rawn* (the old cereal).[7]

The prominence of oats, and to a lesser extent of barley, in the diet of the people of rural Wales in the eighteenth century has been noted by visitors to the country, and this evidence has been corroborated by eminent historians. Thomas Pennant in *Tours in Wales*, describing the welcome he received at the home of the landowner Evan Lloyd of Cwm Bychan near Harlech in 1799, writes:

> He welcomed us with ale and potent beer to wash down *coch yr wden* or hung goat and the cheese compounded of the milk of cow and sheep . . . The mansion is a true specimen of an ancient seat of a gentleman of Wales. The furniture *rude*, the most remarkable are the *cistiau 'styffylog* (or the oatmeal chests) which held the essential part of the provision of the Welsh people in the eighteenth century.[8]

Our forefathers' staff of life at that time was oats, and the general sustenance of the ordinary farmer in Wales during that century was barley bread, oatmeal, *llymru*, *cawl* (broth) and a little bacon. Another author, William Williams of Llandygái, Caernarfonshire (Gwynedd) dealing with the same period, gives a specification for the food of the people living in that part of the country: 'they commonly in farmhouses have three sorts of bread, namely wheat, barley and oatmeal; but the oatmeal they chiefly use: this with milk, butter, cheese and potatoes is their common summer food'.[9] When Benjamin Heath Malkin visited Glamorgan in 1803 he drew attention to the types of bread eaten in different parts of the county: 'I have already mentioned that in the vale all eat good wheaten bread, in the mountains, some oaten bread is used but not so generally as in former times. In Gower, they eat barley bread for the most part.'[10] In his book *A General View of Agriculture and Domestic Economy of North Wales* (1810), Walter Davies criticizes the continued reluctance among the Welsh farming community to grow wheat:

> Thousands of persons who seldom eat any other bread than that of oats and barley, have thousands of acres under their management capable of bearing plentiful crops of wheat but are so accustomed to oatbread that they seem pre-possessed with the idea of the impracticability of growing that superior grain.[11]

However, wheaten bread has not been as important an element in the national diet of Wales as in that of many other countries and it was not generally eaten at the table of ordinary Welsh folk until the later decades of the nineteenth century. The dramatic fall in the price of wheat in the 1880s led to the decline in the eating of oat and barley bread.

Another valuable source of information regarding the foods of the Welsh people during the latter part of the nineteenth and the early decades of the twentieth century is that gained from oral testimony. Details of the preparation and cooking of everyday foods have been handed down orally from mother to daughter, from generation to generation. Evidence, gathered widely from informants in different areas, has revealed that the general sustenance foods of the farming community in Wales at the turn of the century were based on home-cured salt meat, home-grown vegetables, dairy products and by-products, and the main cereal crops, namely oats and barley. The types of bread eaten varied slightly from area to area; it was the general custom to buy imported flour which was added to the home-produced wheat or barley meal to give a better-quality mixed bread (*bara cymysg*). Barley bread of inferior quality, however, was still baked for the menservants in some districts. In the hilly regions, where oats was the only cereal crop grown, the inhabitants would buy all the flour required to make refined bread. Oatcakes continued to be baked, but were now regarded as being supplementary to the home-baked white bread.

FLAT-BREADS AND THE BAKESTONE METHOD

The most primitive method of baking bread was to place small rounds of unleavened dough in warm embers on hot stones or a preheated hearth-stone and allow them to bake until they became hard. Examples of hearth-cakes found at the first-century BC lake-village of Glastonbury survive in the form of very hard small buns. On analysis it was established that they were made of fragments of whole grains of wheat, hulled barley, wild oat, chess and a seed of common orache. There were no traces of leaven.[12] The traditional flat-bread of Wales, oatcake, the common staple since the Middle Ages, was baked by a similar but slightly more sophisticated method and it continued to be a living tradition well into the twentieth century.

The logical development from the primitive method of baking on a hot hearth or flagstone was the use of a thin slab built into and projecting from a wall, sufficiently high to allow for a fire on the ground below, as was found on the site of a Romano-British village in Staffordshire.[13] A similar 'baking stone' was found on the yard of a farm near Llanwrtyd, Breconshire (Powys), measuring twelve inches long and ten inches wide.[14] The portable, circular baking stone is part of this earlier tradition and continued to be in use well into the nineteenth century. Circular iron plates were also introduced in the medieval period and were employed for baking. The Welsh noun *gradell* (griddle) appears in the Laws of Hywel Dda and is included among the iron objects made by the blacksmith.[15]

Bakestones and iron 'planks' are listed in seventeenth- and early eighteenth-century inventories of Welsh landed gentry, yeomen and small farmers alike. A careful inventory of goods in the kitchen at Plas Brondanw, Merioneth (Gwynedd), dated 11 April 1713, includes three iron bakestones,[16] while the inventory (1676) of goods in the possession of William Rowland, a small farmer of Llanfabon, Glamorgan, refers specifically to 'a tripod and one iron plate for baking oaten bread'.[17] A similar reference – 'an iron plank for baking of bread' – was found in the will (1729) of one William John, yeoman of Myddfai, Carmarthenshire;[18] the reference to 'one backinstone' (value one shilling) in the inventory of goods belonging to a William Evan of Pencarreg, Carmarthenshire, is of particular significance.[19]

When employed on a flat-hearth, the bakestone was supported by an iron tripod over the fire. In many areas, however, and more especially in south-west Wales, it was held in position on a circular iron frame with a half-hoop handle suspended from a hook and chain. Other examples of bakestones were made with a half-hoop handle attached to them for suspension. With the introduction of the built-up iron grate or range, it became common practice to rest the bakestone on the two hobs on either side of the fireplace. Peat was recognized as one of the most suitable fuels for heating the bakestone, but coal, wood, furze or gorse, and straw were also used according to local resources.

An accessory tool used in conjunction with the bakestone in Wales was a slender wooden spade or slice. Carved by the male members of the family, it was made specifically for turning the loaves and cakes when baked on the bakestone. The size and shape of the blade varied slightly from area to area, and a similar variation in the Welsh names by which it was known was also discerned. *Rhawlech*, with the variants *awlerch* and *owlerch*, was the general name given to it in Carmarthenshire and Cardiganshire, *sgleish* or *sleish* the equivalent used in Glamorgan and Breconshire, with the name *crafell* used throughout the counties of north Wales. *Crafell* was defined by Thomas Jones (1688) as a 'curry comb, also a wooden slice to turn oatcakes with'.[20]

The bakestone was in constant use in most parts of the country well into the twentieth century. It was employed widely throughout the counties of north and south Wales, primarily for baking unleavened flat-breads, including oatbread and, at a later date, a variety of batter-type cakes. Basically, the ingredients of oatmeal and water and sometimes a little fat were mixed to form a dough which was finally baked on the bakestone.

The art lay in the rolling out of the dough to form large wafer-thin rounds with fine even edges. References to the craft of oatcake-making in historical sources are sparse, and one has to rely on oral testimony to obtain full descriptions of it. It proves that two different methods of rolling out the

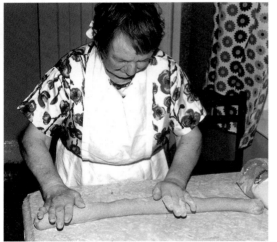

Mrs Mary Davies, Llan-saint, preparing oatcakes, south Wales method: Forming the dough into a long, sausage-like roll.

oatcakes were adopted in Wales; one confined to specific areas in south-west Wales, and the other practised fairly generally throughout the counties of north Wales.

The method of rolling the dough as practised in parts of south-west Wales was as follows. A large piece of dough was rolled out under the palms of both hands until it formed a long sausage-like roll. It was then divided into small equal pieces which were rolled on the table, using a circular motion, one under the palm of each hand, until they formed small balls. These balls were then flattened, one beneath the palm of each hand, and given an occasional quarter-turn (the right hand turning clockwise and the left hand anti-clockwise) until they became equal in size to small saucers. These small, flat cakes, approximately twelve in number, were then placed on top of one another, with thick layers of oatmeal between them, and were flattened still further with the palm of the hand, then with the forearm, giving the whole pile an occasional

Flattening balls of dough into small, flat cakes.

quarter-turn in order to flatten them evenly. When their size had increased to the diameter of a large dinner-plate, they were then carefully separated and any dry oatmeal cleaned off before baking.

In the counties of south Wales the skill was demonstrated by forming a perfectly round, thin oatcake without the aid of a specific tool. This required great dexterity in mixing the dough to the correct consistency, sufficiently pliable for it to be kneaded and flattened with the palm of the hand to form cakes that should be 'as thin as a wafer'. A rolling pin was a common household tool in the nineteenth century, yet it was *not* associated with the art of oatcake-making in south Wales. Without exception the palm of the hand and forearm were the essential

Further flattening of the cakes, with layers of oatmeal between them.

factors. Informants were of the opinion that body heat, radiated through the palm of the hand and forearm, helped to keep the dough pliable so that it could be flattened thinly without cracking. It was the logical conclusion inferred by the experts practising the craft at the turn of the century.

However, it is reasonable to inquire whether the art of using palm and forearm dates back to the period when a rolling pin was *not* an essential kitchen tool. In the Laws of Hywel Dda, comprehensive inventories of furniture and arms in the king's possession are given.[21] Among the kitchen furniture and tools references are found to a griddle, meat-dish, sieve, ladle, a wooden kneading trough and board, but a rolling pin is not included. However *oatbread* is specified in the Laws as part of the food-tithe paid to the king by bondmen and freemen alike. The dimension of the loaves is stipulated – 'let the bread be oaten . . . Six round ones . . . each loaf as wide as from the wrist to the elbow'.[22] Is it not logical to deduce that by using the forearm, from the elbow to the wrist, the flattening and the measuring of the loaf would be carried out simultaneously? This detailed reference given in the Laws, together with the oral testimony collected from informants in specific areas of south Wales, points to the survival of a craft, practised and transferred in its original form from generation to generation, from the Middle Ages to the early twentieth century. Undoubtedly it was a craft created through necessity, and perfected by regular practice.

The craft, however, declined steadily during the first decade of the twentieth century. By this date, in south-west Wales oatcakes were regarded as a delicacy

Mrs Catrin Evans, Cynllwyd, preparing oatcakes, north Wales method: Shaping the dough into a small cone before rolling it out.

Rolling out the oatcakes.

Turning oatcakes with a *crafell* (a wooden slice) and drying them on an oatcake rack.

eaten on special occasions rather than as daily sustenance. Spread thickly with butter they were usually served for Sunday tea. Until the beginning of the nineteenth century oatbread was an essential 'survival food', especially to the small farmer and cottager, but with new developments in agriculture, and gradual changes in the diet of the rural population, its role was changed, and it was thus regarded as 'festival food' for a short period before it became totally extinct. The older generation of women alive at the turn of the century were the last true exponents of the craft in south Wales.

In the counties of north Wales a far more sophisticated method of rolling the dough was practised, and it continued to be a living craft in this part of the country well into the second half of the twentieth century. Details of the method were given by informants from many areas. Using a knife, the well-kneaded dough was divided into equal pieces, which were worked in turn into small cones between the two hands. Each cone was then flattened with the palm of the hand to form a small thick round cake. The cake was rolled out by means of a wooden rolling pin but, again, giving it an occasional quarter-turn for even rolling. Particular attention was given to the edge of the oatcake so that it would not crack. A large thin oatcake, equal in size to a large dinner-plate, with a fine, even edge, exemplified considerable skill.

Baking the oatcakes followed a similar pattern throughout the country. The bakestone would be preheated to a certain temperature which the experienced housewife could easily gauge: 'Oh well, you'd brush it clean to start with, and take a pinch of oatmeal and spread it across the griddle. If it started to change colour, to turn yellow, it was ready. It was hot enough then.'[23] The large thin cake was then deftly placed on the bakestone (griddle). Removed from a pre-hardened batch on the table, it would be carried

> between my two hands like that. Throw it on the griddle. Just two hands each side like that. It was like a penny between your hands. Just put it on the fire, then take the oatcake slice and give it a quarter-turn. Give the loaf a quarter-turn to make sure it baked all over. Then take the slice, look at it a bit, put the edge underneath it and turn it, it was ready. There was no need for it to go a heavy old yellow colour, to bake too much. I liked them to bake a nice clean white. And they were baked enough too, you know.[24]

In north Wales, the cakes were then transferred to a custom-made wooden or iron stand which stood in front of the fire:

> we'd lift them then and put them on the rack. *Car bara* we used to call it. Something like a small screen it was, in front of the fire, with small steps to it, made for the purpose. In front of the fire to finish properly, just in case they weren't done. We'd leave them there for a long time.[25]

Here the cakes were allowed to dry before being stored, usually on top of the oatmeal in wooden chests. In south-west Wales, on the other hand, they were dried in a more casual fashion, resting them against the legs of an inverted three-legged stool near the fire.

In the counties of north Wales, oatcakes were baked on a fairly regular basis well into the second half of the twentieth century. By this date they were often eaten in a sandwich form by placing a large piece of oatbread between two slices of white bread. These 'sandwiches' were given colloquial names such as *brechdan gaerog*, *brechdan linsi*, *brechdan fetel* (a ribbed, linsey or metal sandwich) and *pioden* (magpie). 'Linsey' or 'metal' were technical terms used in

Oatcake label (Museum of Welsh Life archive).

the woollen and slate industries respectively. Linsey was the term used to describe a particular cloth woven from a mixture of wool and cotton, and metal in the quarrying industry was a shale of various colours. These terms were adopted to describe this two-tone sandwich within the communities where these respective industries were prevalent.

They were also consumed in pottage-type dishes, crushed oatcake being the basic ingredient in the dishes known as *brwes* (brose) and *picws mali* or *siot* (shot).

Barley bread was also baked on the griddle or bakestone in certain areas of north-west Wales until the turn of the twentieth century. Prepared specifically to feed the menservants employed on the larger farms, it would be made in large quantities. Although this bread was leavened with yeast it was still considered a flat-bread and to mix a soft, pliable dough was a difficult task. Kneading was the key to its successful baking, a skill taught to every maid hired to work on these farms:

> 'You have to knock hard, you know,' she said, 'for about an hour' – to mix the flour. And then the more you knocked it the tougher it would be, and it would be a better loaf, you see. They'd rise more, the longer you did it. It was a hard job, a farm maid's work, the work of a kitchen maid in those days.[26]

Baking would take place on a flat-hearth in an outhouse:

> And the big griddle then, about three loaves went on this griddle. And the fire would be red-hot. You'd bank it up well the night before baking, and once you'd given it a poke in the morning it would be red-hot. Then bacon fat to rub on the griddle in case the bread stuck to it, and a little bit of barley meal on it afterwards.[27]

The dough was divided equally to form

> large loaves. And they weren't thick, they were something like that – three or four inches then. And round, all of them the same. They were quite uncovered. And to turn them then – an oatcake slice, you know, to turn them. The oatcake slice was a useful instrument to turn bread.[28]

They would be baked evenly for some fifteen minutes on both sides and then placed to cool, leaning against one another, edge to edge, on a stone slab, before storing.

Although the built-in wall-oven was well established in most areas during the early decades of the twentieth century, the tradition of baking on a bakestone coexisted with it. Heating this large oven would be confined to one specific day in every week and subsequently the family's supply of bread and cakes would be augmented by that which could be baked over the open fire. Flat-breads known as *cacen radell* (griddle cake) or *cacen soda* (soda cake) would be prepared and baked regularly in the counties of north Wales, and their counterparts in the southern half of the country were called *bara cri, bara crai* (unleavened bread) or *bara trw'r dŵr* (water bread). On a normal baking day it would be common practice also to bake a small leavened batch on the bakestone, while the bulk of the dough would be baked in the oven. A similar batch, fortified with sugar, lard and currants was another bakestone favourite, prepared in most areas, and was known as *cacen gri* (speckled cake), *teisen does* (dough cake) or *teisen radell* (griddle cake). *Leicecs* (small drop-scones) were baked on the bakestone as a special welcome to visitors in Merioneth and Denbighshire. A variety of pancakes was baked on Shrove Tuesday throughout the country, but more especially in Anglesey and Caernarfonshire where they prepared *crempog furum* (yeasted pancake) or *crempog wen* (a pancake made with refined flour), to be consumed by members of the family, in contrast to the *crempog surgeirch* or *bara bwff* (oatmeal-based pancakes), served to the servants. Occasional labour would be employed in the larger farmhouses on that day to assist in baking a sufficient supply of each type. Pancakes were associated with birthday celebrations in most districts in south Wales, and they were given the names *ffroes*, *pancos* or *cramoth*. Fruit turnovers, and small round cakes, now generally known as 'Welsh cakes', were also bakestone tea-time treats in the southern half of the country.

LEAVENED BREAD

Bread-making was one of the major weekly tasks for which the housewife would allocate a whole day. Tuesdays, Thursdays and Fridays were the regular baking days in different areas. The skill was transferred from generation to generation solely by practical experience. Despite the numerous household-management books published in the eighteenth and nineteenth centuries, it is unlikely that many found their way into ordinary Welsh homes. It was the lore of common sense and experience that governed the quality of bread served to most households. Baking by Welsh housewives followed a very similar pattern in most areas. Taking a large earthenware pan or a wooden kneading trough, the quantity of dough prepared for a week's baking would differ according to the size of the family. The amount of flour used would vary from 7lb to 20lb per baking. By the early twentieth century the majority of households would make bread from purchased white flour, although some informants recalled making mixed bread using a quantity of home-produced wheat or barley flour to fortify the refined flour. All informants noted the important factor of keeping all ingredients and utensils warm throughout the whole process – in the first instance, it was essential to warm the earthenware pan before putting the flour into it.

The type of yeast used varied slightly in different parts of the country. Many recalled using home-made liquid yeast in the rural areas, whereas informants in more urban areas bought liquid brewers' yeast from the local inn. Home-made liquid yeast was prepared in large quantities by individuals anxious to augment the family income. Known as *berman* or *burum dirwest* or *burum total*, it was sold to neighbours for approximately a penny per pint. Its strength was not equal to that of the brewers' or the compressed dried yeast, and this primarily accounted for the custom of preparing the dough in the evenings and leaving it to rise overnight.

> We had an earthenware bowl. A big, earthenware bowl. Earthenware, you know. And then on a Monday night we'd bring the *barm* we'd call it. Yeast hadn't arrived then. *Barm*. We'd get it from the houses nearby. There was an old woman there who made this *barm*, and we'd bring it Monday night

from chapel, and we'd wet the dough. And then, by Tuesday morning, it had risen up, to the top, of course.[29]

Some would pour the liquid yeast and a quantity of warm water into a hole in the centre of the flour, cover and leave it in a warm place to ferment overnight. Others would put the mixture in an earthenware jug and place it on a warm hob for an hour or so to 'prove' before adding it to the flour.

Alternative, less laborious, methods of 'proving' the compressed or dried 'German' yeast, that later became readily available in the local stores, were also noted. One preferred method was to cream the yeast with a little sugar, pour it into a well in the centre of the flour, cover with a little flour and allow it to 'prove' for a short period before proceeding to mix the dough. Another common method was to cream the yeast with a little sugar, pepper and warm water in a bowl, cover and allow it to ferment before pouring it into a well in the centre of the flour. This reactivation of the dried yeast was a sure way of discovering whether it was fit for use.

Mixing the dough followed a fairly general pattern with all informants testifying to the importance of using the correct amount of warm water of 'blood-heat'. Warmer water would ferment the dough too quickly, while hot water would 'kill the yeast' (*lladd calon y berem*). Using too much water, on the other hand, would 'drown the miller' (*boddi'r melinydd*) and give a heavy dough, while too little water would result in a hard bread.

The secret of making good-quality bread, however, lay to a very large extent in the art of kneading the dough. Having gently worked in all the flour into the 'yeasty part', sides to middle, in order to bring the dough to an even consistency throughout, the kneading began. This was hard work. Usually the earthenware pan was placed in a low position, on an old chair, stool or settle, so that the process could be carried out at a comfortable level. Kneading 20lb of flour would take some forty-five minutes. (The English noun 'lady' derives from the Anglo-Saxon *hlaefdige* or 'loaf-kneader'.) Using both fists, the experienced would gently pound the dough, allowing air to enter to make it light and spongy. The secret, according to some, would be to knead 'until the dough sings': the light dough being full of air would squeak as it was handled. The most general observation, however, was to knead the dough until both the hands and the sides of the bowl were free of any loose flour or sticky dough:

> And you'd knead and knead and knead until it was a lump, and there wasn't a bit of dough left around the bowl. The bowl would become clean. Oh, the kneading was important. The more you kneaded the better the bread would be. Then you'd put a fist in it, and cover it with a clean cloth that was quite warm. Then you'd put something over it to keep it warm.[30]

Plunging a folded fist into the perfectly kneaded round lump was also common practice, again allowing more air into the dough as it finally rose in the bowl. Covering the dough in the bowl followed a general pattern, using warm blankets, shawls, newspapers or even overcoats to accelerate the process. Having used compressed yeast, large amounts of dough would take between two and three hours to rise. The bowl would be placed in a warm, draught-free position, usually on the kitchen hearth or on the settle at the side. When using liquid yeast, the process would be allowed to take place overnight:

> And then we had settles at home, each side of the fire, big old settles with high backs to them. And there was a settle here by the side of the fire, and on the corner of this settle the bowl would be left overnight.[31]

By day, another more comfortable position was sought by the inventive housewife:

> And you know what? Old people years ago would put the bowl – the dough – in the bed in the bedroom. And then the bedclothes would go over it like that, and it would rise in no time – after they had got out of their beds! Then it was in – I hope, it was – in a clean place, wasn't it?[32]

The disadvantages of allowing the dough to rise overnight were also noted. One hazard contended with during the summer months was that the dough would turn sour if left in a warm place for too long a period. Another common danger was for the dough to rise too much and consequently fall over the sides of the bowl. When this happened the dough had to be rekneaded, thus delaying the final baking. To prevent this from happening it was essential for the housewife to be up and about very early on bread-baking day!

The final stage of dividing and moulding the dough would be carried out on a large wooden breadboard (*pren bara*) or on the wooden scrubbed-top kitchen table. In the earlier period the dough would be moulded to form large batches for baking on the open hearth. They were baked individually in a greased and preheated pot-oven or beneath an inverted pan on a preheated griddle. With the introduction of the wall-oven, initially loaves were baked directly on the floor of the oven, but informants recalled using old frying pans with broken handles or earthenware pots as bread-baking utensils before tins became available. Both oval and oblong tins were in general use by the post-First World War period. All baking utensils were greased and preheated before use. The dough would be divided and moulded according to the size and number of available utensils. The top of each loaf would be marked with a sharp knife or pricked with a fork to form a symmetrical pattern. Informants were of the opinion that this custom also helped the loaf to bake evenly. To see large holes in the crumb of the bread was no credit to a 'lady'. Finally, the filled tins were placed 'to prove' on the warm hearth for a further half hour before they were placed in a preheated oven.

Simultaneously, some housewives would continue to keep a little dough and bake a small batch on the bakestone. This batch would be eaten fresh for tea on that day. *Bara planc, bara ma(e)n* or *bara prwmlid* were among the regional Welsh names by which this bakestone bread was known. Similarly, small batches would be baked on the floor of the enclosed oven. Regional variations in language accounted for the different names given to them – *bara bricen* (brick bread), *torth waelod popty, torth ar fflat y ffwrn* and *torth llawr ffwrn* (oven-bottom loaf).

Another common baking-day custom was to put aside a small quantity of dough and use it as a base for a currant bread. The usual method was to work a little lard, sugar and currants into the dough and knead it well. It was then covered and left to rise in a warm place, as for bread. Finally it was moulded into a large loaf, placed in a tin and baked together with the ordinary bread. *Teisen fara* (bread cake), *teisen dos cwnnad* (raised dough bread) and *teisen does* (dough bread) were among the more general names given to this favourite loaf.

BAKING

Pan and Griddle Method

An extended use of the bakestone was to employ it in conjunction with an iron pan or pot to form an enclosed area for baking leavened bread. Until the beginning of the twentieth century, it was general practice in Anglesey and on the Llŷn peninsula in Caernarfonshire to bake leavened barley bread beneath an inverted iron pan on the bakestone or griddle. With a tripod-stand supporting the bakestone on the flat-hearth over a low fire, glowing embers would also be piled over the inverted pan, thus enclosing the loaf in a warm chamber. Several bakestones with inverted pans would be used simultaneously on the larger farms. In Anglesey it is known for this particular method of baking to be practised in a sheltered position in the open air, with the bakestone and inverted pan buried in a bed of red-hot ashes. A slow combustible fuel, usually peat, would be used for this purpose, but furze or gorse, straw and chaff were also suitable alternatives. This baking method was described as *pobi allan* (baking outside) or *pobi yn y baw* (baking in the dirt), and the bread itself was known as *bara gradell* (griddle bread) or *bara cetlan* (kettle bread) in Anglesey, and as *bara dan badell* (bread beneath a pan) or *bara padell a gradell* (griddle and pan bread) in Caernarfonshire.

> Pan and griddle, what a baking that was! You had a griddle, a round griddle like the surface of a small table. Then you had something with three legs, a tripod to hold this griddle. And then you'd wipe that clean, and rub it with grease, and then sprinkle a little flour over the whole surface. Then you had a pan, a cast-iron pan – you'd have heated that to start with, you know. And then you'd put the loaf on the griddle and the pan on top of it, and then a good fire. You'd light a fire underneath it, and a fire on top. They used to have turf years ago. That would last a long time. I used gorse, fine gorse, and fragments of gorse – you know the fine stuff that comes from the gorse. Then these gorse fragments were put round it

and on top, and smaller fragments underneath. And that was it, you'd leave it then. Yes, and you'd go there afterwards and look. 'Oh, is it ready yet?' And so that's how we used to use the pan and griddle. Oh, it was a lovely loaf. Much better than an oven loaf.[33]

With the establishment of the built-in cast-iron wall-oven in these two counties during the early decades of the twentieth century, this tradition of baking barley bread was transferred into the oven. The covered loaf was now placed on the floor of the preheated oven. Wheaten bread or mixed-flour bread gradually superseded the barley bread, and the loaves were then baked in upstanding tins in the normal way. Hence the baking-under method in this area became extinct.

The corresponding method employed in north Pembrokeshire and south Cardiganshire was that of using an inverted iron pot or cauldron over the bakestone and the bread was described as *bara dan cidl* (bread beneath the kettle). These two methods of baking, located in the extreme western regions in north and south Wales, can be traced to Cornwall, where two traditional variants on the 'baking-under' method survived into the later years of the nineteenth century. Some households used a 'kettle' – a three-legged iron crock or bowl, others favoured a 'baker', the name given to a plain, round pot which was similar to an outsize frying pan. Whichever type of covering pot was used, the prepared dough was laid on a stout round iron griddle, ready-heated on a trivet thrust into the centre of the open hearth with the burning peat or turf underneath. Having discussed the covering pots in Wales, it is evident that the equivalent of a 'baker' was employed in north Wales and that of a 'kettle' was confined to the southern region.

Pot-oven method
Coinciding with these two traditional variants, however, another baking-pot or pot-oven tradition was evident in the hinterland of Wales. An observer in west Montgomeryshire, writing in 1887 and describing the typical house in the district, states 'weithiau gwneid ffwrn hefyd, ond y rhan amlaf cresid y bara mewn crochan pobi'[34] ('sometimes an oven was built, but generally the bread was baked in the baking pot'). A deep, flat-bottomed pot with straight tapering sides and a closely fitting lid was used extensively for baking bread in Cardiganshire, Carmarthenshire, Merioneth, Denbighshire, Breconshire and Montgomeryshire. Informants from this extensive region of Wales testified that the pot-oven was the only type of oven available until the later decades of the nineteenth century, and that the pot-oven in Carmarthenshire, Cardiganshire and Breconshire was *ffwrn fach* (small oven), while it was known simply as *crochan pobi* (baking pot) in Montgomeryshire and parts of Denbighshire, but the name *cetel* (kettle) was adopted in parts of Denbighshire and in the whole of Merioneth.

The most general method of employing it, usually on a flat-hearth or in a sheltered position outside the house, was to rest it directly on glowing

Baking bread in a pot-oven on an open fire: Mrs Elizabeth Rogers, Ffair-rhos.

embers, or on a tripod over the open fire. Alternatively, the pot was suspended over the fire from a pot-hook and chain. With the introduction of the built-up iron grate, it is known for the pot to be positioned beneath the grate itself, where the glowing embers were raked from the grate on to the lid of the pot. Informants in Breconshire and Denbighshire had witnessed this practice. Baking in the pot-oven was an acquired art, as described by an octogenarian who recalled her own mother's skill: 'Pot loaf. The old lady, my mother, she was exceptional with the pot loaf.'[35] The pot and lid were preheated before placing the risen dough inside it:

> You'd put it to warm, you know, and grease the bottom of it. You'd let it heat up before putting the dough loose in the oven then. You'd make it a small round one, a small round piece, you know. Gosh, it was nice![36]

Peat would be the preferred fuel for use with the pot-oven method, although straw, gorse and wood were again used according to availability. Live embers were placed on the lid of the pot as well as beneath it so that the loaf would be completely surrounded by heat. The building of the embers on the lid had to follow a certain procedure to ensure even baking, allowing an hour or more for a small batch.

A peat fire. I never tried it on a coal fire. The coal fire would go out before it baked, you know. Oh, a small fire. You'd let it burn – to settle, we'd say, you know – let the fire settle before we'd do it. You'd have a red fire to put on the top of the lid and everything then. You had to put a small ring around it, you know. There's a little bit of grooving on the lid of the [pot] oven. Well inside that, you put it round like that. You never put much on the top. Well if you put it in the middle now, the loaf would burn in the middle, you know. The middle rises more doesn't it? You put it on the sides, and it baked the sides and all then. Oh it wouldn't be long, you see. We could only make a small loaf, you see. You didn't make a big loaf, filling the oven. Oh, about an hour and a half, perhaps. That would be quite enough.[37]

Another suitable fuel, used in conjunction with pot-oven baking in certain areas of Wales, was dried cow dung. Available for its collecting, especially during the summer months it provided families with a clean, slow, combustible heat:

My mother's grandmother, in the summer she would go around the fields where the cattle had been grazing, with a stick in her hand and a home-made wicker basket on her arm. And what she'd do if the sun was hot was to take her stick and turn the dung – perhaps it would be a bit damp underneath – and turn it over so that it would dry out. And she'd go back the following day and collect it all, filling the basket. And that's what she had underneath to bake the pot loaf. She'd put this dung under the pot – there was a gap and legs under it – and then she'd make the loaf, put it in, close the lid on this pot then, and put some of the dung on top of the lid. It came over the edges a little. And she'd light that, and then it would heat up. The loaf would bake up and down and on the sides. Baked in the pot, because it wasn't in a tin or anything, you know, and the pot was clean enough. A nice round little loaf. It must have been good, you know.[38]

The pot-oven was gradually superseded by the built-in brick wall-ovens in most houses in the early decades of the twentieth century. Informants, however, recalled their reluctance to relinquish the pot-oven during the period of transition. They referred to the superior attributes of the one loaf which they continued to bake in the pot while the bulk of the bread was baked in the wall-oven.

A distinctive feature of this transitional period was recorded in north Pembrokeshire. An iron pot was placed laterally in a suitable aperture in the kitchen wall, and was fitted with two iron shelves and a custom-made iron door. A fire-box was built beneath it and a flue-vent provided above, thus introducing the *ffwrn gidl* (an improvised pot-oven) as a forerunner to the cast-iron wall-ovens that were later found in the districts of Newport and Brynberian.

BREAD OVENS – TYPES AND LOCATION

The combination of the bakestone and inverted iron pot for baking bread may have been a prototype of the early bread-ovens. Early clay and brick-built ovens were dome-shaped and are known to have been introduced to Britain at a very early date. The Celts, who arrived in Britain during the early Iron Age, used clay domes to parch corn and probably to bake bread. Roman settlers brought further innovations to Britain, including their bread oven. The usual type was a fixed oven with a domed roof of rubble and tiles and a flue in front. Wood or charcoal was burnt inside for a time and then raked out so that bread and cakes could be baked in the heated chamber. In the medieval period, such ovens were to be found in the manor or monastery. The peasant was allowed to take dough to be baked in the manorial ovens on condition that he gave a portion of it in payment.[39]

It is known that wall-ovens, either built-in examples of stone or fire-brick, or more portable ones of clay, were in south-east Wales as early as the beginning of the seventeenth century. The use of the wall-oven spread very gradually to most parts of Wales, but it was not until the late nineteenth century that the baking oven became a common feature in most large farmhouses. However, it seems that the built-in brick wall-oven did not infiltrate as far as some areas in north-east Wales. Farmhouses continued to use the pan and griddle or pot-oven until they had solid-fuel ranges with a cast-iron oven.

A type of portable clay-oven was found in Glamorgan farmhouses in the early seventeenth century. It was a domed structure made of coarse clay banded together with gravel and frequently decorated with applied bands and fingernail impressions. Examples bear a Bideford maker's mark. Bideford in north Devon was the centre of a large-scale pottery industry, in its day rivalling Staffordshire as one of the major British centres of earthenware production. The industry was centred on the three main towns of Bideford, which had a source of gravel still used by the cement industry in the late twentieth century; Fremington, which lay on the band of reddish clay of excellent potting quality; and the port of Barnstable. North Devon clay-ovens were certainly being imported into Wales in the seventeenth century, and were most probably imported a century earlier; the trade continued for a long time, almost up to the time the ovens ceased to be made in the early twentieth century. In 1883, Llewelyn Jewitt wrote in his *Ceramic Art of Great Britain* that the ovens made in the Crocker pottery in Bideford

> are, and for generations have been, in much repute in Devon and Cornwall, and in the Welsh districts, and the bread baked in them is said to have a sweeter and more wholesome flavour than when baked in ordinary ovens.

The last ovens to be produced at the Truro pottery were made in 1937 and were identical to ones made over three centuries before.

The built-in stone or brick oven, however, was far more common than the clay oven in Wales. The earlier examples were found either inside the large fireplace or to one side of it, but examples are very difficult to date. A seventeenth-century date seems probable for the earliest stone or brick ovens in Glamorgan also, except perhaps for the large houses like Beaupre – there is, for instance, no contemporaneous oven at St Fagans Castle in existence by 1590. The early ovens seem to have had thin slabs of stone as a door, plastered around with mud to keep them in place when the oven was in use. They are usually without a flue – in other words the fire was lit inside or hot ashes were used.[40]

However, the built-in baking oven did not supersede the pot-oven tradition in the hinterland of Wales until the late nineteenth and early twentieth centuries. As already indicated, the earlier built-in ovens found in Glamorgan and Gwent were usually located either inside the large fireplaces or to one side of them. This was not always the case in the later, nineteenth-century examples. In Cardiganshire it was recorded that bread was baked in a wall-oven which might be mounted in the wall of the back kitchen or of an outhouse. This outhouse or outside kitchen became a common feature of Welsh life. The separate building frequently housed a baking oven and a copper for boiling water, and it was used for baking bread, washing,

Miss Margied Jones, Craig y Tân, Llanuwchllyn, taking bread to be baked in the farm's wall-oven.

brewing and preparing food for animal consumption. In many areas in north Wales, this building was known as *briws* (brew house) or *tŷ popty* (oven house), while in most parts of south-west Wales it was known as *tŷ ffwrn* (oven house) or *tŷ pair* (boiler house). This terminology variation is evident when it is realized that the general Welsh term for a bread oven in north Wales is *popty* (bakehouse), and its counterpart in south Wales is *ffwrn* (oven) or *ffwrn wal* (wall-oven).

Most of these 'outside' kitchens with built-in ovens seem to be nineteenth century in date and contain an oven with a cast-iron door. Such structures are, however, recorded in south-east Wales from an earlier period: White House, Clytha, Gwent, had an oven in an outside building dating to the late seventeenth century, and there is such a structure, at least seventeenth century, if not earlier in date, at Flemingston in Glamorgan. Indeed, outside bakehouses were common in Glamorgan in the eighteenth century, though, for some reason not yet clear, more bakehouses are known from Gower than from elsewhere in the country. The spread of the outside bakehouse may be connected with the spread of the baking-oven itself.

THE USE OF THE BRICK WALL-OVEN

As soon as the dough had been set aside to rise, the next major task was to fire and heat the oven. To quote William Cobbett in the chapter on making bread in his publication *Cottage Economy* (1822): 'In the mean while the oven is to be heated and this is much more than half the art of the operation.'[41] To heat the oven to the correct temperature was of paramount importance, a skill which was again attained by observation and experience.

The brick ovens were constructed so that each brick was precisely placed to form an arched or a beehive-shaped cavity, the floor of which was also of brick. There were no sharp corners or side flues and the mouth of the oven was closed by a suitable cover or door. The cavity would be filled with dry fuel and, when fired, the flames would encircle the whole surface area.

Housewives throughout Wales continued to follow the same procedure well into the first half of the twentieth century. Primarily they sought sufficient fuel to fill the oven a week in advance so that it could be dried in the warm chamber at the end of a current baking session. Thus, they were confident that it was ready for firing the following week. They could not afford to contend with a damp supply of fuel on baking day.

The fuel most commonly used in Wales was wood – elm, beech or oak being the most suitable, although gorse or broom were known to be used in some hilly regions. However, peat, harvested for use as fuel on many moorland farms, proved more suitable for baking, as stated by a housewife from Llanuwchllyn, near Bala, in Merioneth:

> We had a big oven years ago, heated by peat. Much better a peat fire. Oh yes it was. It heated properly right through. With wood, well, you'd only have little bits of the oven heating here and there. Oh, it would take an hour to heat. And then after it had heated, you had to scatter it all over the oven, spread it out. And then it would turn into red embers, and you'd leave the embers there all across the oven . . . Well, we had something like an old fashioned rake now to spread it about, to scatter the peat. Spread it like ashes over it like this, you know. And then leave it for a bit. And the bricks would have all changed colour and gone white.[42]

The methods employed to determine the exact temperature of the oven varied slightly from one household to another. This informant observed the colour of the bricks inside the oven. White-hot bricks were, in her experience, the key to successful baking. The more general method of determining it, however, was for the housewife to lean slightly towards the oven, push her right arm into the heated chamber and hold it there for a certain number of seconds while she counted slowly from one to ten, or doubling the pace and counting up to twenty. A cooler oven would give heavy, doughy loaves while a hotter oven would provide the family with the inevitable burnt offerings.

Baked bread in a wall-oven, Craig y Tân, Llanuwchllyn.

> Oh, we'd call it the old baking oven, you see. Baking oven. It was an oven made from bricks. It was brick on the inside, and it would redden. You'd fill it, and there was a big roar. A wood fire. You'd keep it full. Then when that had died down, you'd put your hand in to see if there was enough heat there. If you could keep your hand there for about ten seconds, that was enough. You knew it was right then, you see. And then you'd rake the embers out. You had a little thing that we called a scraper. You'd clean the bottom of the oven out then, clean it all until the floor was clean. But the oven was boiling, of course. Hot. And in with the bread then quickly. And shut it and seal it.[43]

Another informant recalls how her mother taught her to 'know her oven' by observing the colour of the wood embers and the colour of the bricks as they rose in temperature, as well as the all-important count up to twenty as the final test:

> You'd light the wood now, and that wood had to burn until the embers were white. And you knew the oven. It would become ready for baking, as the embers died. It would go all white. Inside the oven. White! And Mam now would count to twenty, with her hand on the surface of the oven like this. Twenty. I can see her – hundreds of times counting there. 'That's it, girls. Come on! Ready!' We'd put the bread in.[44]

To remove the dying embers and thoroughly clean the oven floor was essential when all loaves were baked directly on the heated bricks. When tins became available this task did not have to be executed as thoroughly, but if the oven had become too hot, mopping the floor with a long-handled, wet 'dolly' or 'ladi' helped to reduce the temperature. (This tool would be a mop made of rags or sacking.)

'Setting the oven' – the term used for placing the loaves in position inside the oven – was a task that had to be done quickly and smoothly, so that the oven could be sealed as soon as possible thus retaining the heat inside it. Great care had to be taken when handling the risen dough. Each individual tin would be placed on the 'peel' (a long-handled spade-like tool) and placed in position inside the oven. Tins of different shapes and sizes were set like pieces in a jigsaw puzzle. 'You had to know your oven.' Finally, small batches or pot loaves were placed near the mouth of the oven and were later given as baking-day treats to the children.

Ovens fitted with a fixed cast-iron door were readily closed. In this context, housewives frequently referred to the custom of reserving some of the warm embers for use as a 'draught excluder' on the oven ledge, placed tightly against the closed door. This barrier helped to conserve the heat and prevented any cold air from entering the oven.

> Seven loaves of bread. And we'd shut the door on them and leave them there for two hours. An iron door. We'd shut it tight so that no air would get at them. So there was no need to touch the door or anything once the bread was put in.[45]

Earlier brick-ovens, however, were closed with a stone or slate slab which had been cut to size so that it fitted tightly over the mouth of the oven. Informants from many districts, both in the south-east and south-west counties, had vivid recollections of placing these doors in position. To seal or 'pad' around a stone door was another all-important skill acquired by experience. In some households, old rags or paper would be used:

> Plenty of paper everywhere, wetted and squeezed up. It was like putty. And you'd put a real good dab of that all round. Pad the oven. And no air would get in then, you see. It was airtight then. And you know, when you took that down, it was dry. As dry as a bone. But I remember well, I remember having to wet the paper like that. And then, rags after that. Rags would be used very often. You had rags. And they would last longer than the paper, of course. So that was padding. And that was the last task, after the bread had gone in. That was the last task.[46]

When available, clay would be used. It would be easier to handle and was probably found to be a more effective sealer. It also acted as a 'tell-tale', signifying to the housewife the opportune moment to open the oven and find perfectly baked bread. To open the oven too soon could prove disastrous, giving the housewife a week's supply of flat, doughy bread.

> And we'd put the stone, an old stone slab over the oven. And dubbing right around here. Clay, she had to have the clay ready! And the wetter it was, it would dry like a cinder, you see. And you'd see – Mam would say 'It's almost time to take the bread out!' 'How do you know, Mam?' 'Well, you see, that clay is almost completely dry', she said. And she was right! When the clay dried, it was like a cork. It was time for you to open the oven. She was right too. Oh, you can't beat experience. We'd open the oven carefully, and oh, you'd see the bread! Beautiful![47]

The approved baking period varied slightly according to the size of individual ovens, but it usually took approximately one-and-a-half hours to bake a whole batch of bread. The baked loaves were then taken out of the oven again with

Loaves drying out before storing.

the aid of the oven peel. At this stage, it was general custom by most housewives to test each individual loaf as it was carefully removed from the tin. A gentle tap or knock with the knuckles on the sides and bottom crust resulting in a hollow, resonant sound signified a well-baked loaf and a sure reward for their hard day's work. Finally, the loaves were placed on their sides or in an inverted position on a wooden surface and allowed to cool. Freshly baked bread would soon become mouldy if stored while it was warm. Covered with a clean linen cloth, the loaves were usually left to cool overnight and then stored in a suitable receptacle. An earthenware crock or dough bowl with a custom-made wooden lid was chiefly used, although wooden bread-racks suspended from the kitchen ceiling were provided in the larger farmhouses.

The use of the brick oven was not confined to bread-baking. It played a far wider role in a household's economy as indeed it provided more than twenty-four hours' heat. While the bread was in the oven the housewife would promptly prepare some fruit tarts, currant breads and puddings. The bricks retained heat for a long period, but possibly a second, minor firing would be required to boost the temperature before setting the oven for the second time. Furthermore, at the end of the day, a large bowlful of rice-pudding was generally placed in the oven and allowed to bake slowly overnight, a treat enjoyed by all ages. On the following day, the remaining heat was further utilized: the oven now being used as a warm cupboard in which the family's weekly laundry was aired. Finally, it would be refilled with fuel for drying in preparation for the following week's baking marathon.

COMMUNAL AND COMMERCIAL BAKEHOUSES

The tradition of home baking persisted in most Welsh homes well into the twentieth century with members of families strongly objecting to 'boughten bread', commonly known in Welsh as *bara starfo* (bread for starving) or *bara ffenast* (window bread). The built-in type of wall-oven was kept in use in rural areas well into the mid-decades of the century. With the growth of both villages and industrial and market towns, however, cooking facilities in the home changed radically. The small ovens incorporated in the iron kitchen-ranges which were installed in most urban homes in the late nineteenth and early twentieth centuries proved both unsatisfactory and inadequate for baking bread for large families. They were not regarded as 'good bakers of bread'. Reporting on the iron oven in 1855, Eliza Acton wrote in *Modern Cookery*:

> though exceedingly convenient from the facility which they afford for baking at all hours on the day, [they] do not in general answer well for bread, unless it be made into very small loaves or rolls, as the surface becomes hardened and browned long before the heat has sufficiently penetrated to the centre of the dough.

Another domestic economist, writing in a publication entitled *Lady Bountiful's Legacy* (ed. John Timbs, 1868) was of a similar opinion: 'The iron ovens attached to kitchen ranges, in most cases, will spoil the bread attempted to be baked in them as it will be either unevenly baked or altogether burnt.' He stipulated: 'if, therefore, a family possess not a brick oven, the bread should be sent to the baker's'. Esther Copley in *The Complete Cottage Cookery* (1849) advised still further on the economy of using the service offered by the local baker: 'Persons who live near to an honest baker may find it as economical to send their bread to his oven; the usual charge is ½d. a loaf.'[48]

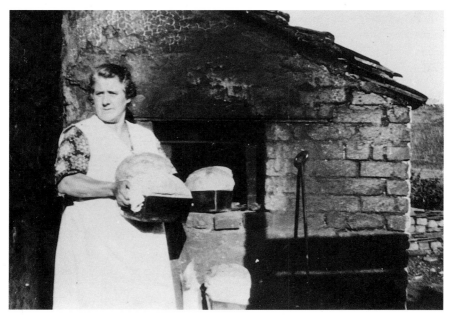

Mrs Susannah Roblings with freshly baked bread at Farrier's Cottage, Rhyd-y-car, Merthyr Tydfil, early 1930s.

Baking day at the village bakery, Llanelidan, near Rhuthun, *c.*1905.

By and large, bakers were not established as commercial traders in Welsh villages and towns until the early decades of the twentieth century. The housewife continued to play a key role in providing bread for the family and was assisted in overcoming the inadequacy of the small iron ovens. In the first instance, builders in urban areas provided communal brick ovens built on convenient sites to serve a specific number of houses only. Ironmasters such as Richard Crawshay, who built twenty-nine houses for the iron-miners of the Rhyd-y-car iron-ore mine near Merthyr Tydfil in Mid Glamorgan in the early nineteenth century, eventually provided three communal ovens to serve this particular community. This arrangement was typical of many streets and areas throughout the industrial towns and villages of both north and south Wales.[49]

In general, these communal ovens were built within a simple, detached, single-storey building, usually located at the end of a terrace of houses. They would be managed in an identical fashion to the domestic models already discussed. Every family would be allocated a specific day when they were granted sole use of the oven situated in close proximity to their home.

> They were bringing their own heating sticks, and they did make a little pile in the middle and they'd put coal around. Inside the oven. And then my mother was keeping the *corlac* [rake] in her back, see, and then before she'd put the bread in, she'd spread it all around with the *corlac* [and] scrape it all out then . . . And she put her hand in then to see 'cause my mother was always baking lovely, and a few used to ask her, 'Come and put your hand in now Mary Ann, to see if it's warm enough.' She knew by the feeling of it, yes. So indeed, the bread was going in then now. I couldn't tell you how long, but she knew the time it was due to come out. Oh, but what beautiful bread it was! Six large loaves. And we used to wait then for us to

have the warm crust off of them. Lovely bread, beautiful bread. And my mother then had a big spade [peel] then to pull them out one by one, see, and then we used to put them on the wall then. The walls were whitewashed. Outside. Everybody, not only my mother. They all used to put them on the wall outside for them to cool a bit before they'd [put them] in a lovely big clean pan in the pantry on the stone, with a big white cloth over it.[50]

An alternative arrangement would be to appoint one man to manage the communal oven which served a specific number of families within the community. He would be paid a set fee, usually one penny per loaf of bread or cake, per baking session.

These communal, end-of-terrace ovens proved to be the precursors of the larger custom-built bakehouses where 'professional' bakers set up business in urban villages and towns to provide the local community with a baking facility. On attaining suitable premises, Welsh entrepreneurs built large brick ovens as commercial enterprises. Customers were invited to bring their home-prepared dough to them and to pay the resident baker for his service.

Derwen Bakery, which was built in Aberystwyth, Dyfed, in 1900 and now is part of the Museum of Welsh Life, represents this type of business. They were established in most areas throughout the country and were well frequented by local residents.

Large numbers of elderly Welsh housewives have vivid memories of their mothers or grandmothers taking advantage of their local baker's oven. Many of them were of the same opinion that to heat up the small iron oven in the home proved expensive; furthermore, it was not 'a good baker of bread'. Using coal to stoke up the oven to attain the required high temperature for the sake of baking a day or two's supply of bread was not profitable. As one commented: 'but it became cheaper to take them to the bakehouse you know. "Communal" you'd call them today. She'd make four at a time.'[51]

Mrs Catherine Jane Evans (née Jenkins) who managed Derwen Bakery until the business closed in 1924.

Another recalled how her mother would depend on the local bakehouse under certain circumstances only: 'Sometimes, when she wasn't well, or perhaps we couldn't have coal or something – not much money – then we'd take the dough, my brother and I, in the clothes-basket, a handle each, to the bakehouse.'[52] A baker's daughter who had assisted her parents in their family bakehouse during the First World War period confirmed that housewives from a large catchment area in the Swansea valley would take regular advantage of the baking facility offered to them:

'Why did these people bring bread to you? Didn't they have ovens?'

'Well, no, I think – it was too much trouble, I think, to heat the oven, you know. And there weren't many gas stoves and electric stoves then, were there? Say around 1916, 1917 like that, there weren't many ovens about. They'd bring about half a dozen loaves, perhaps, and then they would last for the week. And we didn't charge much. We only charged a penny a loaf you see. Yes, and a penny for a tart.'[53]

Many of the successful 'bakehouses' gradually developed into larger commercial concerns, whereby the baker built up his trade by preparing his own dough and baking bread to sell to customers over a fairly wide area. Commercial bakeries were established here and there in the larger Welsh villages and towns during the early decades of the twentieth century. Even at this date, however, many of these bakers still continued to provide the housewife with a baking facility. Side by side with baking his own bread supply, the baker would allocate specific hours or days when he would accept dough from customers for 'public baking'.

Mrs Chris Aston (baker) kneading dough at Derwen Bakery, Museum of Welsh Life.

Having baked his own bread in the morning, one baker referred to the pattern of allocating the afternoon for 'the outsiders':

Well, the batches were out about eleven every morning, about eleven, half past eleven. And the bread out about twelve perhaps, you see. It was all over by about dinner time, see. And we'd bake for the outsiders in the afternoon, you understand. Say – 'bring your bread by two o'clock, make your bread by six, as it suits you,' you see? And then we'd bake tarts for some people.[54]

Other bakers limited their services to certain hours on specific weekdays:

Baking bread at Derwen Bakery, Museum of Welsh Life.

> William Huws' bakehouse, as we used to call it. And we'd bake every –
> wait a minute – Monday and Wednesday with William Huws. Friday
> night, there was a small old bakehouse – you'd get to it through Stryd Bach
> – Robert Jones' bakehouse we used to call it. Friday night, we'd take the
> dough there.[55]

The work area within the bakehouses was sparsely furnished with the basic
requirements for managing the dough and the tins. Cleanliness was of
paramount importance and great care was taken to scrub clean all work
surfaces daily:

> The bakehouse was a sizeable room, with tables right around, of course,
> the shelves. Wooden tables and wooden shelves, and we had to scrub those
> every day, you see. They were like the driven snow, girl. Yes. We would
> whitewash the bakehouse every three months, you know. Whitewash it.
> The walls. And we had red tiles on the floor. We'd wash out every day, and
> the tables were scrubbed every day. And that was the last job we'd do,
> scrubbing the tables and washing the floor out.[56]

Firing these large ovens followed a similar pattern to that already described
for the domestic models, and generally the fuel used was wood. The
experienced baker was also adept at managing and 'knowing' his own oven.
To heat the oven to the required temperature was, of course, a skill gained by
experience only. One baker from Anglesey explained how he knew the oven
was hot enough to use:

> 'There wasn't any kind of thermometer or anything, but you'd do it with
> your hand. You learnt to do it with your hand. You'd open the oven door
> and put your hand in, bare. You knew. When the oven was ready you'd feel

Heating the oven at Derwen Bakery, Museum of Welsh Life.

the heat going like a glove over your hand. It would grasp you. But if the oven wasn't hot, you could hold your hand there for – it wouldn't heat at all. But if the oven was hot, you could feel it moving up your arm, as if someone was putting on a glove. And you'd know that the oven was ready.'

'And what if it was too hot?'

'Well, you'd know that as well. The hairs on your arm would get singed a little. You would know. Then you'd wash it, a bit wetter, to dampen it down a little bit. But, you see, you'd wash it, and as soon as you had washed the oven, you'd put the bread in.'[57]

The later, more sophisticated bakehouse ovens, however, were fired with coal or coke and thus were fitted with a built-in fire chamber beneath or at the side of the oven. Heat would be drawn towards and around the oven and regulated with flues and the temperature recorded on a thermometer usually fitted externally on the oven door.

Carrying the dough from the home to the bakehouse was a delicate task. Having risen in the warmth of the hearth, it would have to be covered with a flannel or thick cloth and carried quickly, as the cold air would check its rising. When the dough was given out to be baked the general custom in the counties of north Wales was to take in one lump and instruct the baker to divide it into specific shaped loaves:

When William Huws, took your dough – it would be in a clean flour sack, with a white cloth around it in case you got flour all over you. Then William Huws would say 'Well how many do you want today? Two or three loaves?' A batch and two tin loaves or two loaves – as we wanted – as Mam had said.

The Arran Oatcakes' Shop, Bala, *c.*1920. (by courtesy of Gwynedd Archives)

> It was like a big kitchen. You – where the oven was – and I'm talking now about where he used to handle the dough and cut the bread into tins – one side like this was clean tins. And you know it was necessary to grease each tin, in case the dough stuck to it, wasn't it? Well now, one side was like that, it had these tins. Each one ready for its loaf. Then, along here there was a big, long table where he took the dough and cut it. It was a white table like the snow, too, and he had plenty of flour on it when he was cutting the dough.[58]

The preferred pattern in the counties of south Wales, on the other hand, was for customers to mould the dough at home and place it in tins before taking it to the bakehouse. These loaves were readily identified by both the baker and the customers alike:

> We'd put every loaf on top of its own tin, you know. In case there'd be a mistake. Say now, some people would bring their own bread in to be baked, you understand. Some would mark their tins, of course, you know. They'd put D.J. or A.R. or something like that. Then you knew who was bringing the bread by the tins, you see. And you'd put the loaf that had been baked on top of that tin, you see. You'd take it out of the tin and put it on top of the tin, otherwise it would sweat when it was left inside you see, and it would go soft. And we'd take every loaf out of its tin and put them on top of these tins there on the table. And they'd come to fetch their bread afterwards of course.[59]

The baker who took in customers' dough for moulding and baking in his own tins also devised a foolproof method of identifying all the individual customers' bread:

And, you know, it was comical – everybody knew and recognised his own dough! Why? you say. When William Huws took your dough he would – he had a tin, like a loaf tin, and that full of tallies. Then he would give you a tally, and put – if you had three loaves, he'd put a tally on each loaf. Then he had a tally just the same to give to me as well. Then when we went to get the bread, 'The tallies with this number, look!' There were like six tallies, you see. In each pile, each one had six. Then, there'd be a number, you see. Say there was 1, 2, 3 on the three that went into our bread – well, we'd have three tallies to go home with, 1, 2, 3. He knew then that those were our loaves, you see'.[60]

However, some customers would have their own method of identification despite the baker's tally system.

And Gran would take a piece of paper like this, and write her name – Margiad Wiliam – put it in the side of the loaf. And there were tallies to be had. They'd give you tallies. But Gran didn't have much faith in tallies. She wanted to put her name, Margiad Wiliam, on the bread. She'd make four at a time.[61]

Setting a large oven was a major task which had to be accomplished at great speed. Individual bakers had their set methods according to the types of loaves baked together in the one baking session. One baker described his method of using a long-handled peel to put the loaves in position:

'You'd start in one corner. You had to have a system, you see. And then you came along the side. Then you worked across and forwards until you'd come – it takes about a quarter of an hour to twenty minutes to fill it. It did. And that as fast as you could do it. Tins first, and then by the door there'd be the small loaves and cobs and brown bread and pan loaves.'

'And what about the batch loaves?'

'Well, they were in the centre of the oven, in the middle of the tins. You had to have a plan for filling it, you see. You filled it like that until it was square. Then it looked really beautiful!'[62]

Baking fees were minimal but they provided the baker with a well-earned income. A penny a loaf was quoted as being the normal charge at the turn of the twentieth century. Baking Christmas cakes, however, proved a little more expensive:

'We only charged a penny a loaf, you see. Yes, and a penny for a tart. And for a pudding too. But Christmas cake – Christmas started three weeks before Christmas in our house, because the cake was being baked, you know. And people bringing their cakes there. It would be a loaf cake. They'd bring about half a dozen loaves at a time, you know. Some would bake their cake very early. And others, later, of course. Some would bake their cake about three weeks before Christmas, while others would do it nearer Christmas, you see.'

Owen (D. W. Teviotdale) Bakers with their horse-drawn bread-carts, North Parade, Aberystwyth, c.1915. (by courtesy of Stewart Williams Publishers, Barry)

'And baking that would cost more?'

'Yes, tuppence. Tuppence.'

'And they would take longer to bake, of course.'

'Oh yes, I'll tell you, we'd put the first lot in at six o'clock in the morning. Cakes at Christmas time now. Then we'd bake again at ten, and again at four perhaps. We'd finish then. And we'd do that say – Father would watch that the oven wasn't too hot, you see. Say now, Tuesday, he wouldn't bake a Christmas cake at all, because it was too hot. Well, it had cooled down a bit by Thursday and Wednesday, you see. He'd bake some on a Wednesday and a few on a Thursday. So that the cake wouldn't burn, because a rich cake like that burns more easily than bread, you see, doesn't it? Yeast cake most people made for Christmas, you see.'[63]

Children played a prominent role in transporting the dough to the bakehouse and collecting the bread at a given time:

Oh yes, we'd always take the bread to William Huws after dinner, on the way to school. And then we'd leave the flour sack and the white cloth there ready. We'd go home to have tea first, then we'd take the basket – we had a clean clothes-basket – to fetch the bread. And then . . . the sack that had held the dough and the white cloth would always have been rolled up by William Huws. And put in the middle like that. Then the loaves, after he had taken them – they had always cooled a bit by the time we had them – were put like that, and like that, in the basket. And then there were two little white cloths. We'd be one at each end holding the basket, and this little white cloth would go over the bread. And the thing that had carried the dough to the bakehouse was in the middle, of course. Yes.[64]

Another informant recalls calling at the bakehouse after school in the afternoon and being given a special treat by the baker. She and her brother having taken the dough to the bakehouse in a clothes-basket on their way to school, they would return to collect the loaves on their way home:

> It would be a penny a loaf for baking them. And we'd carry them home in the basket. And in case we started to make holes in the loaf, trying to eat on the way home from school, Dic would make a small loaf for us. Yes, he would. For my brother and myself. From the dough. On the sly that was.[65]

Bakehouses at the turn of the century were not regarded solely as workshops or business places, they also served as community centres. Like the cobbler's shop or the village smithy, the bakehouse was a popular place for social gatherings. Young girls and boys would meet there as they went to collect their bread. A baker's daughter recalls this happy time:

> 'Oh dear, dear, that was a lovely time. And you know, it was a happy time, when the people used to come in to get their bread. Oh, Mam would shout at me, "Come on, you've been long enough chatting out there now!" The girls coming in, you know, and the boys coming in to fetch – they'd make it an excuse, you see, to come into the bakehouse to have a chat. Yes, to have a little chat and a little gossip, you know. Oh, a happy time.'

> 'Did they have somewhere to sit down?'

> 'Yes, we had a bench, you see. We had a bench to sit down. Yes. That's it – all the gossip then, you see. And Mam losing her temper then, of course!'

> 'Was the place open till late at night then?'

> 'Well, say until around eight o'clock, nine o'clock.'[66]

Children were known to have long ears at that time, as always, and were not given a very warm reception at such gatherings:

> 'There was a social side to the bakehouse, I'm sure, was there?'

> 'Oh yes, certainly. And do you know, a crowd would collect, having left their dough there – we children going to school weren't able to stay, but when we went to collect the bread there was some fun. And we used to like to stay and listen. And I remember a very amusing character used to come to Robert Jones' bakehouse. He's been dead for years, poor thing. He was a painter. Oh, he'd tell some tales! And we wouldn't want to go from there with the bread. And sometimes they were things we shouldn't have heard, as children! Old Miss Jones and Robert Jones would throw us out on those occasions.'[67]

The old brick oven has played a prominent role in the lengthy story of bread-making. From Roman times to the early decades of the twentieth century, the texture of its bread was second to none. The oven's special attributes are described by an Anglesey baker:

'You were telling me earlier that there was quite a difference between an oven like this and the modern electric ones. What is the difference?'

'Oh, well, the old brick oven, it draws some water – the bricks draw the water. But these modern ovens, the water goes back into the loaf. Because of the metal. It throws it back. And so the crust doesn't break like the crust of an old brick-oven loaf. The crust of an electric-oven loaf, it wants to stretch. That's the difference. Like glass and cotton wool, say.'[68]

Many commercial bakers in Welsh towns and villages continued to use their old brick ovens well into the first half of the twentieth century. Some were converted so that they could be fired with coal, coke or gas. Others were replaced by more sophisticated models with side or back furnaces, which were also fitted with external thermometers. Small family businesses grew as transport facilities improved, more especially in rural areas, in the immediate post-Second World War period. Bakers' vans travelled a radius of some ten to

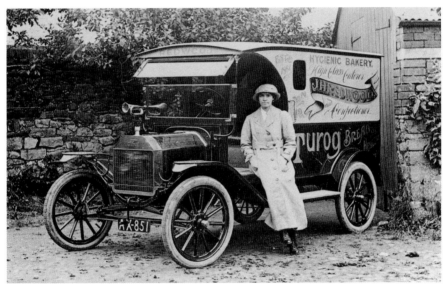

J. H. Redwood, Abergavenny, delivery van, c.1914. (by courtesy of Stewart Williams Publishers, Barry)

fifteen miles to deliver freshly baked bread to both village shops and isolated farmhouses and cottages. On average, the baker became a regular visitor to most rural areas two or three times a week. This service led to the gradual decline of the art of home baking. Having experienced a flour shortage during the war years, housewives readily purchased bread which was delivered to their doorstep. Coincidentally, many of the old brick ovens were falling into disrepair and were thus abandoned or covered up.

The story of today's factory-produced bread is very different. Baking methods may have improved, but what of the quality of the bread? The constant demand for loaves baked in the old brick oven of Derwen Bakery at St Fagans is answer enough. There is *no* baking like the old baking!

NOTES

[1] Sir Richard Colt Hoare, Bart (ed.), *The Itinerary of Archbishop Baldwin through Wales* by Gerald de Bari (London, 1806), vol. 2, p.289.

[2] Ffransis G. Payne, *Yr Aradr Gymreig*, (Caerdydd, 1954).

[3] Stephen J. Williams and J. Enoch Powell, *Cyfreithiau Hywel Dda yn ôl Llyfr Blegywryd* (Caerdydd, 1942), p.69.

[4] Leslie Alcock, 'Some reflections on early Welsh society and economy', *Welsh History Review*, 2 (1964), 4.

[5] Hoare, *The Itinerary of Archbishop Baldwin through Wales*, pp.292–3.

[6] George Owen, *The Description of Pembrokeshire*, ed. Henry Owen (London, 1892), vol. I, p.33.

[7] Ibid., pp.59–61.

[8] Thomas Pennant, *Tours in Wales* (London, 1810), vol. II, pp.276–7.

[9] William Williams, *Observations on the Snowdon Mountains* (London, 1802), p.7.

[10] Benjamin Heath Malkin, *The Scenery, Antiquities and Biography of South Wales* (London, 1807), p.544.

[11] Walter Davies, *A General View of Agriculture and Domestic Economy of North Wales* (London, 1810), p.358.

[12] C. Anne Wilson, *Food and Drink in Britain* (London, 1973), p.230.

[13] John Ward, *Handbook to the Exhibition of Antiquities* (National Museum of Wales, 1913), p.15.

[14] Museum of Welsh Life (hereafter MWL) MS 1793/290, Mr Evan Jones, Ty'n-y-pant, Llanwrtyd.

[15] Williams and Powell, *Cyfreithiau Hywel Dda*, p.98.

[16] Bob Owen, 'Plas Brondanw', *Journal of the Merioneth Historical and Record Society*, 3 (1957), 255.

[17] National Library of Wales, PR (L1), 1676.

[18] William John, Myddfai, Carms. Will, 1729 in NLW.

[19] William Evan, Pencarreg, Carms., 1714

[20] Thomas Jones, Amwythig, Y *Gymraeg yn ei Disgleirdeb* (Llundain, 1688).

[21] Williams and Powell, *Cyfreithiau Hywel Dda*, p.98.

[22] Ibid.

[23] MWL tape, no. 2832 (trans.), Mrs Cathrin Evans, Cwm Cynllwyd.

[24] Ibid.

[25] Ibid.

[26] MWL tape, no. 3987 (trans.), Miss Jane Catrin Williams, Rhosbeirio.

[27] Ibid.

[28] Ibid.

[29] MWL tape, no. 3064 (trans.), Mrs Ann Mainwaring, Margam.

[30] MWL tape, no. 2946 (trans.), Mrs Elizabeth Roberts, Bryncroes.

31 MWL tape, no. 3064 (trans.), Mrs Ann Mainwaring.

32 MWL tape, no. 2946 (trans.), Mrs Elizabeth Roberts.

33 Ibid.

34 I. C. Peate, 'The pot-oven in Wales', *Man*, 43(1943), 9–11.

35 MWL tape, no. 3839 (trans.), Mrs Elizabeth Rogers, Ffair-rhos.

36 Ibid.

37 Ibid.

38 MWL tape, no. 2688 (trans.), Mrs Laura Davies-Jones, Llanbedr.

39 Eurwyn Wiliam, '*Yr Aelwyd*: the architectural development of the hearth in Wales', *Folk Life*, 16 (1978), 85–100.

40 Ibid., 85–100.

41 William Cobbett, *Cottage Economy* (Oxford, 1979), pp.48–71.

42 MWL tape, no. 2831 (trans.), Mrs Cathrin Evans.

43 MWL tape, no. 3064 (trans.), Mrs Ann Mainwaring.

44 MWL tape, no. 3088 (trans.), Miss Cissie Davies, Tonyrefail.

45 MWL tape, no. 2831 (trans.), Mrs Cathrin Evans.

46 MWL tape, no. 3065 (trans.), Mrs Ann Mainwaring.

47 MWL tape, no. 3088 (trans.), Miss Cissie Davies.

48 Elizabeth David, *English Bread and Yeast Cookery* (London, 1977), pp.155–88.

49 E. William, *Rhyd-y-car: A Welsh Mining Community* (Cardiff, 1987).

50 MWL tape, no. 7090, Mrs Janet Davies, Rhyd-y-car.

51 MWL tape, no. 5871 (trans.), Mrs Elizabeth Evans, Blaenau Ffestiniog.

52 MWL tape, no. 4409 (trans.), Mrs Margaret Jones, Llanrwst.

53 MWL tape, no. 4648 (trans.), Mrs Anita Rosser, Llansamlet.

54 MWL tape, no. 3975 (trans.), Mr Alfred Price, Aberffro.

55 MWL tape, no. 3978 (trans.), Mrs Edith May Hughes, Llannerch-y-medd.

56 MWL tape, no. 4648 (trans.), Mrs Anita Rosser.

57 MWL tape, no. 3974 (trans.), Mr Alfred Price.

58 MWL tape, no. 3978 (trans.), Mrs Edith May Hughes.

59 MWL tape, no. 4648 (trans.), Mrs Anita Rosser.

60 MWL tape, no. 3978 (trans.), Mrs Edith May Hughes.

61 MWL tape, no. 5871 (trans.), Mrs Elizabeth Evans.

62 MWL tape, no. 3974 (trans.), Mr Alfred Price.

63 MWL tape, no. 4648 (trans.), Mrs Anita Rosser.

64 MWL tape, no. 3978 (trans.), Mrs Edith May Hughes.

65 MWL tape, no. 4409 (trans.), Mrs Margaret Jones.

66 MWL tape, no. 4648 (trans.), Mrs Anita Rosser.

67 MWL tape, no. 3978 (trans.), Mrs Edith May Hughes.

68 MWL tape, no. 3974 (trans.), Mr Alfred Price.

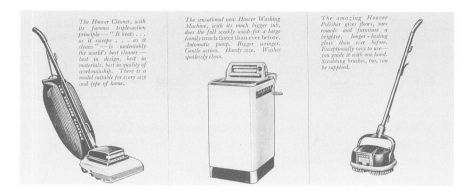

The Hoover Cleaner, with its famous triple-action principle — " It beats . . . as it sweeps . . . as it cleans " — is undeniably the world's best cleaner — best in design, best in materials, best in quality of workmanship. There is a model suitable for every size and type of home.

The sensational new Hoover Washing Machine, with its much bigger tub, does the full weekly wash for a large family much faster than ever before. Automatic pump. Bigger wringer. Gentle action. Handy size. Washes spotlessly clean.

The amazing Hoover Polisher gives floors, surrounds and furniture a brighter, longer-lasting glass than ever before. Exceptionally easy to use— you guide it with one hand. Scrubbing brushes, too, can be supplied.

Going Electric:
The Changing Face of the Rural Kitchen in Wales, 1945–1955

> I'm glad that I have lived to experience the best of two worlds: the pre-electric era with its open hearth and peat fire, and now the convenience of modern-day appliances, the press-the-button era![1]

This quotation is from a letter written by a female correspondent from rural north Wales in 1987. By and large, nearly forty years had elapsed by then since electricity was brought to rural Wales, and it therefore seemed that the time was ripe to capture the memories of the housewives who had experienced the excitement of having this new 'clean' power brought to their homes for the first time. They would be the only informants who could assist the social historian to realize the significance of the changes it brought with it. What were the revolutionary effects of having electricity in the rural home? How quickly did it change the daily work-routine? Did this 'magic power' change the mode of cooking in Wales overnight? Did it become a prime factor in causing the demise of traditional foods?

To find the answers to these questions the author published a short article in the daily and weekly press throughout Wales in 1987, appealing for readers' responses. A monetary award was offered for the most informative and interesting letter giving an account of the correspondent's experiences and recollections of 'going electric' in his or her home. A collection of some thirty letters were received. They are representative of different areas of both rural north and south Wales, and provide sufficient pointers to some definite patterns and trends which occurred in ordinary cottages and farmhouses with the introduction of this new 'energy'.

Firstly it will be appropriate to recapitulate briefly the traditional methods of cooking. In Wales in the seventeenth century, as in the other countries and regions of Britain, cooking on the open hearth was the only method and was common to all households, both rich and poor. This method continued to be dominant in Wales throughout the eighteenth and nineteenth centuries and, indeed, prevailed in many rural households well into the twentieth century.

Boiling in an iron pot or cauldron to provide cereal or meat-based pottages continued in rural Wales during the early decades of this century; both the pot-oven and the bakestone were employed extensively for baking bread, cakes and pancakes, and spits, bottle-jacks and Dutch ovens were used for roasting fresh meat. The open fire with its appliances was adequate to fulfil the cooking and baking needs of most rural households. The general introduction of the built-in wall-oven to the larger farmhouses, during the second half of the nineteenth century, facilitated the major weekly operation of baking bread, but its use was confined to this one day in every week.

Mrs Margaret Maddocks, Upper Cornelly, baking round cakes in a Dutch oven on an open range.

The second phase in the general evolution of cooking methods was the development of the open range in the mid-eighteenth century. It was marked by a transition from a wood or peat fire on the flat-hearth, or in a simple iron grate, to a more elaborate iron range. Movable iron trivets were attached to the grate's upper bar to support a tea kettle or other small utensil. The size of the fire could be altered or adjusted by contracting the sides or 'cheeks' of the grate or by folding down its front bars. By the 1860s, open ranges usually included side-boilers for heating water and ovens for baking, heated by conduction or by a system of primitive flues. It was not until the late nineteenth century that these ranges were established in ordinary homes in Wales, and even at that date they were confined to the industrial towns and villages where coal was the main source of fuel. With their eventual introduction to rural areas in the early decades of the twentieth century, the use of their small ovens was restricted to the cooking of the weekend joint; they did not replace the large wall-ovens for bread baking. Midweek cooking continued to be carried out over the open fire with the cast-iron boiler or saucepan, frying pan and bakestone in constant use.[2]

Concurrently with the open fire and open range, one other stage in the evolution of cooking technology must be mentioned. Paraffin-oil cooking-stoves became available to the rural housewife in Wales during the late 1920s and early 1930s. These stoves proved popular in many homes and gave Welsh cooking a new dimension.

A number of different models of oil cooking-stoves were produced in the nineteenth century, primarily in North America and especially in the west where settlers had managed up to this time with an open fire and a brick oven. They began to be marketed in the 1830s and became available in Britain for the Great Exhibition of 1851. It was not until the great Paris Exhibition of 1878, however, that the prototype of the 'modern' paraffin-oil stove could be shown to the public by Besnard and Maris, the latter being already famous for their excellent and popular paraffin lamp.[3]

Many different designs of these small, inexpensive cooking-stoves were marketed in England and Wales during the early 1920s. They remained in use in many areas of Wales throughout the 1940s, and in some instances they were still favoured well into the 1950s. They were inexpensive to buy, and paraffin oil was readily available in local stores; it was already purchased to provide lighting in most rural homes. Therefore, to the more ambitious housewife, tempted to experiment with a new mode of cooking, this new stove was revolutionary. To have some form of regulated heat enabled her, to quote from one advertisement, 'to make meals to delight the family'. Until then she had been restricted to the open fire and a brick or cast-iron oven with the emphasis on slow cooking.

One of the most popular models of the stoves marketed in England and Wales was known by the trade-name *Valor – Perfection*. It was manufactured by the Anglo-American Oil Co. Ltd, and was sold by reputable ironmongers and hardware stores. An advertisement for this particular model was published in the 1920 edition of Mrs Beeton's book *Family Cookery*. It stipulates:

> Built to save time, work and worry, the *Valor – Perfection* stands supreme.
> It has new double-wall chimneys that concentrate all the cooking heat

where it is required . . . A tender, juicy roast, vegetables perfectly cooked, sweets so delicious that they melt in the mouth, no wonder the family are proud of Mother's cooking and she of her wonderful *Valor – Perfection* Oil Cooking Stove.

The author qualifies as a daughter of one of these proud owners of a Valor cooking-stove. My mother purchased one during the 1940s and continued to use it well into the 1950s. I recall the roast dinners and delicious puddings cooked in the oil-stove! I also remember how my mother experimented with cooking 'new' cakes such as light Victoria sponge cakes, queen cakes, and maids-of-honour in this new oven. Until then, these dainty delicacies had not been seen on the tea-tables in rural homes. Gradually, birthday parties and church or chapel teas were given a new image with decorated sponge cakes and other colourful dainties appearing alongside the more traditional fruit breads and griddle cakes.

Of course, these stoves were not without their disadvantages. They posed a fire hazard, and without constant vigilance the wicks smoked and emitted an unpleasant smell or fumes. Great care had to be taken to keep the stove perfectly clean and it was not to be stood in a draught. As Mrs Beeton noted, 'if proper care is exercised, excellent results may be obtained'.[4] According to written reports, however, of all the families lacking both gas and electricity supplies in 1948, 60 per cent chose coal as their cooking fuel and only 23.5 per cent chose paraffin oil.[5] Even so, the oil-stoves ruled supreme in many a rural home in Wales well into the 1950s.

By and large, electricity did not reach the farmhouses and cottages in rural Wales until after the Second World War, and had no real impact until the early 1950s. (In the context of this study, we shall not be looking at the history of establishing electricity boards and what was involved in bringing this clean 'non-solid fuel' to rural areas.) After the initial excitement of acquiring this new energy in the home, what were the revolutionary effects that followed? Today, it may be difficult for the young housewife to appreciate fully the marathon task of keeping house without the usual labour-saving electrical appliances at her elbow. It is natural for us to assume that, in the first instance, every housewife would have rushed out to the nearest supplier to buy an electric cooker. Surely, this clean appliance with an easily regulated source of heat would have rapidly superseded the wall-oven, the cast-iron range (or by this date, the Aga or Rayburn solid-fuel closed ranges) and of course, the smelly oil-stove. What could be easier than switching on the electric oven to provide all sorts of goodies? No more mess and no more guessing. Consequently, it would soon change the diet of the rural population in Wales. The true story is gleaned from the correspondents' observations and recollections.

On reading the letters received, it is obvious from the outset that cost and availability of ready money were major ruling factors. Here are some leading quotations:

1950s advertisement for electrical equipment. (By courtesy of Angex Ltd, Europa House, London)

We did not rush out to buy electric appliances immediately, money was scarce in those days – we had to weigh the pros and cons before we ventured out to the shops.[6]

Money was rather scarce – there was no temptation to lash out on all the latest electrical goods.[7]

We had electric light, we were too poor to buy any electric gadgets.[8]

Indeed, it soon becomes apparent that, because of the cost factor, it was a matter of priorities and, seemingly, in most homes, first priority was given to lighting. As one correspondent noted:

Wiring the house cost us £150 – a fortune in those days. But what luxury![9]

Other correspondents reiterated the same remarks:

> In the home, to have a light in every room was the most important item. The Aladdin oil lamp was no longer required in the living-room and we were no longer dependent on candlelight to move from room to room. The thrill of switching on the light in every room was tremendous.[10]

> Light – that was the first priority. Away with the oil lamp and the temperamental Aladdin lamp along with the nightly ceremony of lighting it. Away with the flat enamel candleholders – the dim candlelight and the dripping candle grease. Yes, it is the light that I most vividly recall.[11]

One informant wrote of a package, which was on offer with the North Wales Power Co. Ltd, whereby a house was wired for four light fittings and one 5-amp plug, free of any initial monetary outlay for the householder. The cost would be recouped through a coin meter. She writes:

> So we had an electric supply. One light in the parlour (used on Sundays only), one in the best living-room and one each in the bigger bedrooms. The paraffin-oil lamp remained in nightly use in the kitchen (the busiest room in the house), but one member of the family had the bright idea of running a 'flex' from the front living-room down through the passage and into the kitchen, a distance of at least some 10 yards. And so it remained for years![12]

To have an electric light in every room was indeed a great advance, but of course, it had to be used sparingly; a 25-watt bulb was the average strength of bulb in use. A 40-watt bulb gave a very strong light and was expensive to use!

> Mother was horrified if lights were left on throughout the house, and the usual questions asked were 'Do you really need this light on now?' or 'You have left the light on in such and such a room,' followed with a directive to switch it off immediately.[13]

Following on in the line of priorities, what appliance had second place? It is again clear from reading the informants' letters that, of all the modest affordable appliances on the market, the housewives' first purchase was an electric iron:

> I suppose, like most people, the first electric appliance my mother bought was an electric iron. Even this was an innovation being able to swish over the clothes without putting flat irons on the fire and not getting iron mould marks on the clean linen.[14]

> The first gadget which my mother bought was an electric iron. It was very useful, especially in the summer. She didn't have to light a fire to heat the two flat irons. No more black smuts dropping from the iron on to the clean white shirts![15]

To see a rack full of well-laundered items of linen airing above the fireplace was the pride and joy of most housewives, and consequently a clean appliance to assist them with this time-consuming chore was eagerly purchased.

Another affordable appliance high on the priority list was a vacuum cleaner. Many informants recalled house-visits from representatives of certain firms or stores who were employed to travel around rural areas to sell vacuum cleaners. They would demonstrate the magical attributes of this wonder appliance by throwing a handful of sand or dust on a mat. Members of the family were invited to observe the performance and of course were amazed to see the dust disappear instantly! A typical quotation:

> The next item was the vacuum cleaner. This had a tremendous advantage over the brush and dustpan or Ewbank sweeper and the usual removal of mats for shaking and beating out-of-doors. I still feel today that the vacuum cleaner is one of the most effective labour-saving devices, and one to which newly-weds give priority.[16]

Although one could argue that fitted carpets were unheard of in most farmhouses in the early 1950s, and stair carpet was a luxury afforded only by the most well-to-do farmer, this appliance was readily purchased to ease the burden of cleaning the home. To be clean was to be respectable, an important standing among most Welsh married women.

Next in line in many a home was a mains-operated radio. Early after the Second World War, world affairs were still of paramount importance to the head of the house, and the frustration of having a news bulletin fade away in mid-sentence was no joke!

A new wireless – that was an important change. No more carrying the wet battery to town every Saturday for re-charging and bringing the other one home. It was a relief to know that you could listen to a whole programme without fear of it fading away completely, or even worse, the sound hovering half-way through a programme, picking up a few words now and again as the battery was running flat.[17]

Wireless in the 1955 Rhyd-y-car cottage, Museum of Welsh Life.

Another small appliance high on the list of modest purchases, according to some, was an electric kettle. Despite the reluctance of some housewives – one of whom recalled that 'there was no need to buy an electric kettle, we always kept the iron kettle on the boil over the open fire'[18] – the more innovative saw the advantages of purchasing this useful appliance at an early stage:

If the fire was low, waiting for the kettle to boil was infuriating, not forgetting that one got his hands filthy dirty every time one touched the old black kettle.[19]

It can readily be deduced from the informants' letters that to contemplate such a major purchase as an electric cooker had to be given serious consideration. It has already been noted that cost was a very relevant factor, as is openly admitted:

> My mother's greatest ambition was to own an electric cooker, but this large purchase was governed by finance so she had to wait for this item. Eventually, the day dawned when the wonderful Jackson cooker was delivered.[20]

However, it becomes evident that there were other considerations that outweighed the cost factor in many instances. People's aversion to change cannot be ignored. The following two quotations are significant:

> Mother was always the last one to want new equipment and change.[21]

> We had our farm wired in 1933. My parents left the farm in 1953 having not changed any of the cooking appliances. Mother still liked to do all the cooking on the iron range. She didn't have an electric cooker, electricity did not change our diet. A good supply of *cawl* (broth), bakestone cakes and *teisen lap* (light fruit cake) to the end![22]

Farmwives were not the only ones to adhere to old methods:

> Our council house was the lap of luxury after the cramped cottage. There were lights in every room, even in the toilet. Power points too predominated, but as yet, we were slow to use them. Cooking? I still preferred to use the coal oven which was attached to the open grate. An electric oven came much later.[23]

Other correspondents reported that they had remained faithful to their solid-fuel closed-range ovens for cooking. They could not fault the Aga, the Rayburn, the Yorkseal for fulfilling all their family needs.

Tradition dies hard. Even the more innovative during the pre-electrical period – the housewives who had purchased an oil cooking-stove – were not prepared, at this stage, to discard their favourite stove and replace it with an electric one. To many, the oil cooking-stove had become part of the traditional scene and they had no reason for changing it.

> A cooker? We had a Valor oil-stove since I was a very young girl. We used it daily. I remember more than one coming to our house over the years. It was ideal for roasting, baking and making fancy cakes. There was no need to change it for an electric one. We kept it out in the shed in winter but it was brought into the house in summer when the fire was not lit.[24]

Another correspondent was of the same firm opinion:

There was no electric or gas stove to beat the Valor double-burner paraffin cooker for baking a sponge cake. It took me years to cast it away and purchase a second-hand Baby-Belling electric cooker.[25]

Tradition or not, however, by the mid-1950s many electrical companies were well prepared to capture the consumer market; the drive was on to sell major domestic electrical appliances. The early electric cookers were not attractive to look at, nor were they easy to keep clean. They were cast-iron, ugly black monsters. One of the leading pioneers in the field of electric engineering was R. E. B. Crompton. Electric ovens made by Crompton and Co. were first demonstrated in 1891 at an electrical exhibition at Crystal Palace, London. By the 1900s, there were several companies manufacturing cooking apparatus.[26]

C. R. Belling encouraged the use of electricity by marketing his smaller cookers. In the mid-1920s, Belling brought out the prototype of the famous Baby Belling, a small table-model with an oven and a single boiling-plate and grill. In 1935, a Baby Belling cooker with an oven and one small hob could be purchased for under £4. It was around this period also that electricity began to compete seriously with gas for cooking in urban areas, but electric cooking assumed little importance nationally before it was made available to the rural housewife in the early to mid-1950s. According to published reports, only 6 per cent of families in Britain had an electric cooker in 1936, and 18.6 per cent in 1948. Thereafter, the figure rose to 30 per cent by 1961 and 46 per cent in 1980.[27]

What were the marketing tactics taken to convince or even brainwash the rural housewife that for her cooking needs she should at least consider changing to electricity? By the mid-1950s, reputable magazines were carrying large advertisements with eye-catching captions. A prize example appeared in *Good Housekeeping* in 1953, with the leading caption:

I'd never go back from Electricity to old-fashioned cooking now!

One of the key words highlighted in this advertisement was *clean* (see p.117). It was very relevant to impress on the housewives of that period that it would not only be easier to cook by electricity, but it would also cut down on many other time-consuming chores which were associated with the old-fashioned methods. Housewives in general strove to keep the house clean under fairly difficult circumstances. Some were accused of being houseproud to the degree that cleanliness was next to godliness! To be given the opportunity to purchase a cooker which would also cut down on many of the other dirty chores would be worthy of serious consideration.

By the mid-1950s, well-known manufacturers of electrical domestic appliances were publishing colourful promotional leaflets and posters which became readily available to the rural housewife at local showrooms. An excellent example was published by Belling and Company Ltd, Enfield,

1950s advertisement for electrical equipment. (By courtesy of Angex Ltd, Europa House, London)

Middlesex. The main introductory heading read: 'Belling, the perfect cooker' – with three highlighted sub-headings:

gives new confidence – this is the oven to make a doubtful cook a confident one, knowing that well prepared food put in this oven will be cooked as you wish it to be – perfectly . . .

so clean – when you've finished cooking see how easy it is to clean – a wipe over with a soapy cloth is usually sufficient – there are no fumes or flames to cause a sticky deposit on the sides and bottom . . .

so certain – and most wonderful of all, you can be certain of the same perfect results every time, thanks to the thermostatic control . . .[28]

Today it is impossible to assess the impact that this kind of promotional material had on rural housewives but, again, the correspondents, amongst their recollections, have divulged some definite clues as to how they were eventually persuaded to change their mode of cooking. Initially, representatives of local firms were called in to wire the farmhouses and cottages for a mains electricity supply, and it would usually transpire that they were in league with an electrical appliances' supplier or hardware shop. The lady of the house would then be persuaded to visit the showroom or shop where she was able to see the sparkling new cookers. She was given the opportunity to inspect and admire them, and made to realize that they were available for a small cash deposit.

Pressure was also put on mothers by their young daughters who were now taught cookery as a subject in secondary schools. Here they became familiar with using an electric cooker during their weekly lessons. Eventually, they pleaded with their mothers to become more modern in the home. One informant wrote of the thrill of having electricity in their village in 1957: 'I was only twelve years old and I still recall the thrill to know that we were modern, at last!'[29] Keeping-up-with-the-Joneses was another relevant factor. Competition between neighbours within a small village has always been keen, as this informant admits:

As we all had electricity at the same time, housewives tended to emulate each other and buy whatever appliance the next-door neighbour would have already bought. Miss Thomas next door bought an electric cooker and as soon as she was happy with using it, Mother bought one too. After that there was no need to carry paraffin from the shop for the old oil cooker. At last that went out to the shed, in case it would be needed again some time. But we still used the old iron frying-pan over the open fire for quite a long time after buying the electric cooker.[30]

However, it seems that the most influential marketing tactic was a far more direct and practical one than those already discussed. Regional Electricity Boards appointed suitably qualified ladies as 'demonstrators', who were given specific areas within which they were to work. They were expected to travel around villages to find a suitable venue where they could demonstrate to potential customers the real advantages of owning these new appliances. To demonstrate fully the use of a cooker, they were asked to prepare and cook a variety of dishes, and maybe entice the ladies with the end product: the tactic of 'The proof of the pudding . . .' A very informative letter was received from one lady who, in 1949, was appointed demonstrator by the South Wales Electricity Board in south-west Wales. She was given a very large rural area within the Lampeter–Tregaron region and she recalled:

The hours were long from 9 a.m. very often on to 10 p.m. as I gave demonstrations both in the afternoons and evenings, cooking, also washing and ironing. It was my duty to produce appetising dishes, and keep up a high standard of cooking. And also to provide 'sales-talk'. It was important to sell hard at a terrific pace, holding demonstrations and exhibitions at whatever village which had been connected with electricity, usually in schools or village halls. The drive was on![31]

This lady's letter is proof enough to show how effective these practical sessions were, and how the demonstrator could even influence members of her audience to purchase her own favourite make of cooker.

I, myself, had bought a small cooker, a 'Jackson Giant', in 1949 – a small one that worked off an ordinary plug. This new, small cooker had two radiant rings plus a hot plate, the latter, I had to emphasise, was more expensive to use, but the ladies were thrilled to have it for baking the traditional Welsh cakes and pancakes. As I had one at home, I really did excel in demonstrating with the 'Jackson Giant' and, consequently, the sales soared. I remember whilst holding a week's demonstration at Tregaron Hall, the Boss called me to his room one evening and told me off in no uncertain terms, that if I was to carry on like that, all the other cookers would be left unsold![32]

Following a demonstration session at a certain location, the demonstrator would be 'on call' in that area for the next two weeks. She was expected to make house-visits and give after-sales advice to customers, as required. A number of new appliances were known to have minor teething troubles at that time. This lady's experiences are informative:

The customer's first major purchase after attending one of these demonstrations was usually a cooker. All the housewives had their large fireplaces and wall-ovens or anthracite coal cookers such as the Rayburn, but they bought the electric cooker to use for special cooking when temperatures could be so accurately controlled. They were used for cooking rich fruit Christmas cakes – using a low temperature for a long cooking period. Also for baking meringues and other fancy cakes. They were also used for baking pastry when a really hot oven was required. Housewives eventually became aware of the high cost of stoking up their coal-fired cookers, also the wasted heat that escaped up the chimney on a windy day. But, for the sake of keeping the electric oven clean, meat was usually roasted in the coal-fired cooker.[33]

Electricity therefore was still regarded as being too expensive for cooking ordinary dishes. Initially, it was used for selective cooking only. The demonstrator recalls her experience of visiting the home of a senior bank official who had purchased an electric cooker: the housekeeper was busily boiling jam on one of the electric hobs. All was well until the bank manager arrived home, unannounced, to find jam boiling on the electric cooker. He was infuriated and demanded that the power was switched off immediately. Electricity was far too expensive to be wasted on boiling jam!

> I had to try and calm him down by demonstrating the 0–10 simmerstat. Though he was well up in finance, it took me a long time to explain how a thermostat worked. It was beyond his IQ![34]

Many of the electric cookers were found to have been fitted with faulty thermostats and had to be taken back to the local suppliers for readjusting. Consequently, a house-visit would be arranged and the appliance fully tested in the customer's home. One such occasion is recalled:

> On one occasion, a very wealthy lady had phoned for me. In order to prove to her that her cooker worked properly she gave me a long list of different things to bake. She wanted her cooker fully tested and I spent four hours cooking at her house. Next day, another lady rang up the office asking for the 'demonstrator' to call at her house. She too produced her list and kept me busy for four hours; it turned out that she was a friend of the wealthy lady. She confessed later that she was throwing a party that evening![35]

It appears that some people were not diffident in making the system work for them even in those seemingly innocent days. During her house-calls, the same demonstrator found instances where the electric cooker was used simply as a store cupboard. Many housewives were nervous of using these new appliances even though they had taken the very positive step of purchasing them. Others lacked a suitable place to accommodate the new cooker in their kitchens, and consequently it was kept in reverent seclusion in the front room or parlour, where it remained unused!

In the course of this study it became evident, as this lady demonstrator admitted, that the transition from cooking over the open fire and solid-fuel ranges to electricity proved to be a lengthy procedure. It was the small electric models like the favourite 'Jackson' or 'Baby Belling' that eventually accelerated the change. The size, versatility and low purchase price made them attractive to all types of households. The purchase price of an ordinary Baby Belling in 1957 was £8 12s. The promotional leaflet boasted:

Baby Belling stove in the 1955 Rhyd-y-car cottage, Museum of Welsh Life.

> It works off *any* power point, no special installation needed. Will cook a full three-course meal for less than 2d.[36]

Having familiarized themselves with these small cookers, ordinary housewives gradually appreciated their advantages in comparison with the traditional oven. Ultimately, they bought larger, more sophisticated models. The price of solid fuel also escalated steadily, thus making the running costs of an electrical cooker less prohibitive. But it must be emphasized that the mode of cooking and diet in rural Wales did not change overnight. The change from pottages boiled over the open fire to casseroles cooked in the oven, the change from bakestone cakes to fancy cakes baked in a regulated oven, was a very gradual one.

It is fitting to review the change in the pattern of housekeeping in rural Wales from 1945 to 1955 as revealed in this collection of letters. With the intro- duction of electricity to a rural home, the Welsh housewife primarily purchased modestly priced appliances which literally eased the burden of housework. Cleaning the house was a back-breaking marathon task and until then there were virtually no labour-saving devices. Ironing the family weekly wash with a flat iron was both time-consuming and soul-destroying when an item would be inadvertently soiled with black residue on the base of the flat iron or scorched with an overheated one. Her first purchase, therefore, was an electric iron followed, in second position, by a vacuum cleaner. How does this choice fit in a wider, more national pattern? Published reports reveal that:

> Apart from lighting, most households only used electricity for two functions: ironing and occasional space heating. By 1948, 86 per cent of households had electric irons and 64 per cent electric fires: 40 per cent owned a vacuum cleaner, 19 per cent a cooker, a mere 4 per cent had a washing machine and 2 per cent a refrigerator.[37]

Some ten years later, the same pattern emerges in rural Wales. Space heating was not a problem where there was a plentiful supply of solid fuel, thus the vacuum cleaner took second position. The electric cooker followed much later, as did the washing machine, refrigerator and other smaller luxury appliances like toasters, coffee percolators and so on. As one writer aptly stated: 'Time puts everything in its place.'[38]

Finally, there is one other set of comments which punctuate many of the correspondents' letters and cannot be ignored. In retrospect most of the correspondents do not deny the progress and benefits which they experienced with the advent of electricity. As one housewife readily admits: 'Running a home today is child's play with the magic of electricity.'[39] On reflection, others tend to be rather more sceptical:

> Whilst it is still a thrill to make a new purchase, I feel perhaps we have all become a little blasé about new electrical inventions. There is not that uncertainty and excitement there was in the old days, but that is progress, I suppose![40]

They also acknowledge that electricity gave the housewife more liberty and free time. As one elderly informant pointed out: 'My daughters are completely dependent on their many appliances, from food mixers to central heating. They have more leisure time.' But then she asks the question: 'Is domestic life better now?'[41] This next writer enlarges on a similar theme:

> We have much more leisure, but we have lost some of the quality from our lives in the process, for not only did the mechanism of our chores change, but also the whole way of life. Community life changed too.[42]

She stipulates that:

> It was not long before aerials sprouted on the village roof-tops. The weekly visit to the cinema lost its attraction. People did not make their own amusements. The chapel and the WI meetings were not the centre of entertainment any more. 'Americanisms' crept into our speech . . . Electricity changed our whole lives far more than we anticipated at the time.[43]

Another writer reaffirms the same sentiments: 'Electricity brought a great deal of change on the hill. The rural community was pushed out.'[44]

Like most innovations, this new power was a mixed blessing. The opening phrase of the quotation used as an introduction to this chapter serves also as an apt conclusion. As that lady wrote:

> I'm glad that I have lived to experience the *best* of two worlds . . .[45]

Unfortunately, one cannot have only the best all the time.

NOTES

[1] Museum of Welsh Life (hereafter MWL), MS 3537/15 (trans.), Mrs Margaret E. Jones, Cricieth.
[2] S. Minwel Tibbott, *Cooking on the Open Hearth* (National Museum of Wales, 1982).
[3] Doreen Yarwood, *The British Kitchen* (London, 1981), p.92.
[4] Mrs Beeton's *Family Cookery* (new edition, London, 1920), p.97 and advertisements section.
[5] Geoffrey Browne, *Patterns of British Life: A Study of Certain Aspects of the British People at Home, at Work and at Play, and a Compilation of Some Relevant Statistics* (Hulton Press, London, 1950), p.106.
[6] MWL MS 3537/7 (trans.), A. L. Jones, Lampeter.
[7] MWL MS 3537/20, Mrs Joyce Roberts, Wrexham.
[8] MWL MS 3537/3, E. Erasmus, Newbridge, Gwent.
[9] MWL MS 3537/19 (trans.), Mrs Glenys Roberts, Mold.
[10] MWL MS 3537/1 (trans.), Mrs Carys Briddon, Machynlleth.
[11] MWL MS 3537/23 (trans.), Mrs Heulwen Thomas, Defynnog.
[12] MWL MS 3537/26, H. Williams, Abergele.
[13] MWL MS 3537/14, L. Jones, Bala.
[14] MWL MS 3537/2, Mrs Joan F. Donoghue, Rumney, Cardiff.

15 MWL MS 3537/1 (trans.), Mrs Carys Briddon.

16 MWL MS 3537/2, Mrs Joan F. Donoghue.

17 MWL MS 3537/23 (trans.), Mrs Heulwen Thomas.

18 MWL MS 3537/19 (trans.), Mrs Glenys Roberts.

19 MWL MS 3537/1 (trans.), Mrs Carys Briddon.

20 MWL MS 3537/2, Mrs Joan F. Donoghue.

21 MWL MS 3537/6, C. G. Curtis Jenkins, Cardiff.

22 MWL MS 3537/24, D. J. Walters, Glynneath.

23 MWL MS 3537/20, Mrs Joyce Roberts.

24 MWL MS 3537/19 (trans.), Mrs Glenys Roberts.

25 MWL MS 3537/17, Dafydd Evan Morris, Denbigh.

26 Anthony Byers, *Centenary of Service: A History of Electricity in the Home* (Electricity Council, London, 1981), pp.22–7.

27 Caroline Davidson, *A Woman's Work is Never Done: A History of Housework in the British Isles, 1650–1950* (London, 1982), p.71.

28 *'Belling' 47AB the perfect cooker* (illustrated colour leaflet).

29 MWL MS 3537/1 (trans.), Mrs Carys Briddon.

30 Ibid.

31 MWL MS 3537/10 (trans.), E. M. Jones, Lampeter.

32 Ibid.

33 Ibid.

34 Ibid.

35 Ibid.

36 *Belling Electric Heating and Cooking* (1957–8; illustrated colour leaflet).

37 Geoffrey Browne, *Patterns of British Life*, p.104.

38 MWL MS 3537/7, A. L. Jones.

39 MWL MS 3537/3, E. Erasmus.

40 MWL MS 3537/2, Mrs Joan F. Donoghue.

41 MWL MS 3537/20, Mrs Joyce Roberts.

42 MWL MS 3537/27, Mrs Elizabeth Williams Ellis, London (originally Pencaenewydd, Caerns.).

43 Ibid.

44 MWL MS 3537/6, C. G. Curtis Jenkins.

45 MWL MS 3537/15 (trans.), Mrs Margaret E. Jones.

Modesty, Protection or Display?
The Covering of Table Legs in Wales

If one could step back into the 1860s, into a living room characteristic of the mid-Victorian period, one would immediately be aware of an enclosed, dark atmosphere. Heavy mahogany furniture and thick, velvet curtains would dominate the room, with white lace curtains covering the windows, and tall geranium plants, strategically placed on the window sill, providing further protection from the outside world. A sofa and two armchairs, probably in dark green or brown upholstery, would add to the comfort within the room, and an occasional table and a piano, all in dark wood, would bear some carved decoration. Clutter and drapery was characteristic of the middle-class Victorian living room. Manuals on home improvement in the mid-1860s specifically instructed readers not only to drape their doors and fireplaces, but also to provide the maximum space for 'things'. Indeed, a lack of clutter was considered bad taste.[1]

Drapery and covers would be very prominent, giving the lady of the house plenty of scope for her love of needlework. There would be tablecloths and runners, antimacassars and cushions. There were fringes for the edges of mantelpieces, valances for the sofa and frilly skirts to cover up the knees and legs of machine-carved piano cases.[2] Dust-covers for the best parlour or covers for everyday use in living rooms were common, to be removed only when guests were expected.[3] Drapery for doors was illustrated in house-keeping manuals. Such was the Victorian horror of exposing anything that even some fireplaces were framed with curtains.[4] An obsession with 'dressing' a room was clearly evident during this period.

The above description would have been true of a modest middle-class home at any time during the latter half of the nineteenth century, for fashion in furniture style and interior decorating does not change overnight. Furniture was inherited from generation to generation and most people grew up surrounded by an interior decoration which was almost that of a generation before their own. This was true of the Edwardian period when women's magazines and housekeeping manuals strove to introduce 'better' and simpler taste in furnishing and decorating the home. Mrs Flora Klickman, the editor of *The Girls' Own Paper*, noted in 1911 the paradox found in Edwardian interiors: the fashion leaders voted for simpler and less crowded rooms, but the majority of upper- and middle-class people preferred fussy decoration, thickly furnished rooms and surfaces crammed with knick-knacks. Such an interior is denounced by the editor:

> Where a house is one succession of fancy mats and drawn-threaded cloths and expensive table-centres and a multiplicity of doilies, then it becomes bewildering and gives one a stifled look . . . It has become the custom to smile pityingly at the mention of the mid-Victorian antimacassars that decorated every chair in the best room, but many houses today are just as unsuitably over-decorated with needlework.[5]

Despite the drive to promote clear spaces instigated by the Arts and Crafts movement during this period, the majority of living rooms were dominated by clutter which, according to some authorities, reached its highest density in Edwardian times.

The Victorian clutter and love of 'dressing' a room reached lower down the social scale. A study of the interiors of terraced houses in the industrial valleys of south Wales during the late nineteenth and early twentieth centuries shows how strongly established and persistent it was. Throughout the nineteenth century, observers noted that the people living in the densely populated industrial town of Merthyr Tydfil in Glamorgan were excessively proud of their household possessions and lavished immense care on their houses whether they owned them or not. All but the poorest houses were literally crammed with furniture, pictures, ornaments and knick-knacks. Some articles of furniture were regarded almost as fetishes – the mahogany chest of drawers, for example, or the fire irons, or porcelain figures. This was particularly true of the highest class of workmen's houses consisting of some five rooms. It was in such households that the desire for emulation and the joy of possessions could be most readily satisfied. A typical kitchen-cum-living room in this type of house would contain a mahogany chest of drawers supporting an eight-day clock, a looking-glass and other articles designed for display rather than use, including a clasped folio bible. On the walls, coloured prints of noble personages, famous events or topics of religious interest would be prominent. There would be a mahogany table and chairs, and the mantelpiece, draped with a mantle valance, would support the more cherished articles of polished brass.[6] The womenfolk took enormous pride in their homes and kept them spotlessly clean and neat in total contrast to the filthy conditions outside. Such houses undoubtedly set the standard for houses lower down the social scale.

A small terrace of six industrial workers' houses was removed from Rhyd-y-car near Merthyr Tydfil in Glamorgan and re-erected in the 1980s at the Museum of Welsh Life's open-air park. These ironworkers' houses were built during the first decade of the nineteenth century by Richard Crawshay, the iron master, to his own special design. On site at the Museum they have been furbished and furnished to represent six specific periods within a time-span dating from their original erection c.1800 to the year 1975 when they were finally abandoned because of a flood disaster.

The Rhyd-y-car houses were built on a very much smaller scale than the five-room house whose living room has already been described. The terrace consists of modest, two-storey houses with only two rooms on the ground floor, and a small stairway leading to one open room above. Fortunately, members of the Museum staff were able to interview former occupants of some of these cottages, and thus gain invaluable information. One of the informants, born in 1902, was a lifelong inhabitant of the terrace until its demolition in 1979.[7] She spent her formative years in her parents' home which was only a few doors away from her grandparents' house. On marriage, she and her husband were fortunate to have possession of the house next to her original home. An octogenarian, she was able to recall in great detail the contents of her parents' house. The interior of the house as she remembered it during the 1920s and early 1930s was typical of a very modest working-class interior in an industrial town in south Wales at that period. She describes an over-furnished living room, crammed with furniture, ornaments and drapery. The hub of the room, naturally, was the brick fireplace with a small cast-iron oven at the side. The fireplace and oven were purely functional, but of the utmost importance to the informant were the surrounding ornamental accessories. The high mantelpiece, draped with a chenille valance, was decked with a pair of Staffordshire china dogs and numerous pairs of brass candlesticks of graded sizes. To add to the glitter, a brass clothes airing-rod and smoke hood, a brass fender and hearth trivet and a brass-lidded kettle adorned the hearth. In a strategic position directly opposite the front door, and in full view of all casual visitors, were the best or 'fetish' pieces of furniture. A mahogany chest of drawers stood supreme, clothed with a crocheted runner and adorned with a clock and a pair of tall vases. A framed mirror was suspended on the wall above it. A highly polished mahogany table stood alongside the chest. Covered with a chenille tablecloth, it supported the brass-clasped family bible. The ornate legs of the table were covered with long woollen stockings. A dark upholstered sofa was in line with the table, again clothed with an antimacassar, cushions and valances. The functional half of the room, out of immediate view, accommodated a scrubbed-top table, benches and chairs. All the daily household chores could be accomplished within the boundary of this half of the room. Here, the family would also partake of their meals. The other half of the room, referred to by the informant as the 'best side', was set aside to accommodate the family's proud possessions. Although deprived of a separate 'best room',

The 'best side' in the 1925 Rhyd-y-car cottage, Museum of Welsh Life.

these less-privileged families strove to own and display items of furniture that were obviously regarded as status symbols.

This interior of the 1920s had many Victorian and Edwardian characteristics. Dark mahogany furniture covered with fringed cloths, crocheted runners, antimacassars and valances proved that the love of 'dressing' a room persisted. But, during the interview, the unusual facet of this 'dressing' emerged. While referring to the venerable treatment given to the prized items of mahogany furniture, the informant elaborated on a remarkable custom practised in most of the Rhyd-y-car houses during the 1920s. The ornately turned legs of the polished mahogany table would be covered with woollen stockings. Long, knitted, Welsh woollen stockings, once worn by the male members of the family, were adapted to cover and protect the legs of the table. They would be removed on special occasions only.

Covers for table legs? Was this another Victorian custom which the Welsh housewife had inherited from her ancestors? Did it reflect modesty, protection or display? How widely distributed was this custom in Wales during the early twentieth century? Lacking relevant documentary evidence to corroborate this custom of covering table legs, the oral evidence from Rhyd-y-car, Glamorgan, instigated further research. In 1985, a short letter appealing for information regarding table-leg covers in Wales was circulated to the press and was published in both English and Welsh weekly papers throughout the country. Some forty written replies were received, and a follow-up questionnaire sent to each correspondent seeking more detailed information. Oral evidence was also collected from members of four local history societies in specific areas in south-east Glamorgan and Gwent, and in south-east Dyfed. The remainder of this article is based on the information gained from these sources.

Of the written replies, fourteen were received from Mid Glamorgan, five from South Glamorgan and eleven from West Glamorgan. The remainder were sporadic examples located in the industrial areas of Dyfed, in the slate-quarrying districts of Gwynedd and in the industrial, coastal areas of Clwyd. The few examples that emerged from the agricultural areas of Dyfed were found to have had some family connections with the coal-mining valleys of south-east Wales. (Two isolated examples from industrial Staffordshire and the West Midlands were also recorded by English immigrants now settled in Glamorgan.) The survey undertaken strongly suggests, therefore, that the custom was a feature of the industrial valleys of south Wales, with a few exceptions in larger detached farmhouses in rural areas and in small cottages in the slate-quarrying areas of north Wales. The informants' evidence indicates that the covers were in vogue during the 1920s and 1930s with only a few examples being in use as late as the 1950s and 1960s. One exception was recorded for 1972. It was also noted that the custom was generally practised by the very proud, middle-aged or elderly housewife and that, by and large, it was discarded when their generations passed away. Other elderly informants recorded that the custom was abandoned when the husband retired from the colliery or when the children had grown up and left home. The younger generation following in their mothers' footsteps, in some instances, were known to have varnished the table legs regularly, for protection. With the change in furniture style during the Second World War, the plain, slender legs of the utility-type table did not warrant covering.

TYPE OF TABLE

In the confined, one-room situation of the Rhyd-y-car houses, where both the 'best' mahogany table and the pine scrubbed-top table were housed within the same room, leg covers were fitted on the 'best' table only. In the small terraced house consisting of a kitchen-cum-living room and a separate front room or parlour, leg covers were usually fitted on the table in the living room where the family partook of their meals and also sat during their leisure hours. The housewife would also be confined to this same room to fulfil most of her household tasks. The type of table most commonly used in this situation was a pine, scrubbed-top table with turned legs.

The parlour would house the 'best' table, usually of mahogany (1900s–1920s) with highly polished, slender legs, or of oak (1930s–1940s) with bulbous legs. In both instances, the legs would be hidden with covers. In the larger terraced house, a middle room, located between the kitchen and parlour, would possibly relieve the parlour of its large 'best' table. In this situation, parlours would be furnished with a smaller table which would be left uncovered provided that the room was kept out of bounds to children and pet animals: such parlours were hardly used at all.

TYPE OF COVERS

The distribution of the types of covers used does not follow a geographical pattern. The various types available were common to all areas and were as follows:

Cretonne covers used to protect table legs at Hirwaun, near Aberdare, between 1890 and 1920.

- old, knitted knee-length stockings, in grey, brown or black wool, usually previously worn by the male members of the family. Feet removed, hems would be sewn on both ends, through which tapes or elastic would be drawn for securing the covers around the table legs;

- custom-made covers of chintz, cretonne or damask material with tie-strings. In many homes the old woollen-stocking covers were used in the kitchen, while the custom-made, more decorative types were confined to the middle or front room. However, it was not unusual to have the stocking-type in both rooms. Other homes would boast chintz-type covers in the living room and progress to the damask-type ones in the middle or front room;

- brown paper tied around the table legs and filled with mothballs (in rural areas only);

- short, custom-made crocheted pieces to conceal the lower, turned decoration only;

- ladies' nylon stockings recorded in one instance only where the custom was kept until the early 1970s.

REASONS FOR USE OF TABLE-LEG COVERS

It is apparent from the survey that the covers were used, first and foremost, as protection during the early decades of the century. Table legs were very vulnerable when surrounded by large families in a small, confined room. They were exposed to many injurious factors, of which the most threatening were the miners' or quarrymen's hobnailed boots. Playful children wearing strong boots or shoes were also prone to kicking table legs, and cats had a habit of sharpening their claws on the bulbous, turned decoration at the base of the legs. Covers protected them from being defaced in any way. However, it was noted that the most functional types would be removed on special occasions. The woollen stockings would be removed on a Saturday if the family was entertaining the local preacher for meals on Sunday. Other distinguished guests such as 'important' relatives or professionals such as the family doctor, would be given the opportunity to appreciate the bare, decorative legs. Family gatherings such as weddings, christenings and funerals would also qualify for a similar unveiling. On the other hand, the more decorative custom-made covers would be removed only briefly for laundering. The table legs themselves would also be polished during this brief exposure.

ORIGIN OF CUSTOM

It is difficult to trace the origin of this custom in the industrial valleys of south Wales and, to a lesser degree, in the industrial areas of north Wales. Do we detect here a relic of the 'Victorian horror of exposing anything'? Furniture historians have noted that it was characteristic of the Victorian period 'to conceal the natural beauty of polished wood deliberately by cloths and covers'.[8] They have also drawn attention to the irony of the Victorian compulsion for covering beautiful tables in sitting rooms with heavy cloths which hung in luxurious folds to the carpet. 'A leg, it seems, was something to be concealed, whether constructed of wood, or of flesh and bone.'[9]

To date, no documentary evidence is available to corroborate the use of custom-made table-leg covers in English homes during the Victorian period. However, photographs illustrating Victorian drawing-room interiors show heavy cloths purposefully draped to conceal the legs of tables. Young girls, who left south-east Wales during the late Victorian period to find work, are known to have been employed in service in fashionable homes in England. They would have witnessed these luxuriously draped cloths concealing table legs. Returning home on leave they would naturally have described the fashion to their mothers. The wives of industrial workers would not have been able to afford the lavishly long tablecloths, but possibly they would have accepted, in theory, the fashion of concealing the table legs. It is feasible that they would have used their initiative by making separate covers, which could be secured with drawstrings beneath their own shorter chenille table-covers.

Informants who witnessed the custom in practice during the 1920s and 1930s stressed that it was kept by elderly housewives only. These ladies may have been bearers of a tradition which was originally part and parcel of Victorian modesty. This theory may be verified by the following remarks quoted from one informant's letter:

> Grandmother had a horror of seeing bare furniture legs. My grandmother had a horror of any bare legs on furniture, the table and chair legs, were covered.[10]

On the other hand, table-leg covers may have been part of the Victorians' obsession with 'dressing a room'. Clutter and drapery, as mentioned earlier, would have been characteristic of a middle-class Victorian interior of about 1860. Comfort was certainly a priority in homemaking during that period. The theory suggested by some scholars is that the darkness created by dark furniture, heavy curtains, drapes and so on was intentional in order to ward off the increasingly uncomfortable outside world.[11] The housewife strove to create a congenial atmosphere, paying particular attention to neatness and orderliness which were essential to the comfort and wellbeing of all the members of the household. This atmosphere was noted by an informant who witnessed such an interior in a terraced house in a south Wales valley in the 1930s. Drapes and covers are prominent in the following description:

> The kitchen table legs were covered with a pretty flowered print. They looked like long drawers beneath the plush cloth; also the sofa had a valance and cushions of the same flowered print, plus the two fireside armchairs. I thought it all looked very cosy.[12]

However, it is possible that table-leg covers were devised solely for protection. Living under harsh conditions in the coal-mining valleys during the 1920s, the Welsh housewife dedicated her whole life to keeping a clean and respectable home for her family. She constantly strove to ward off the ubiquitous coal dust that polluted the whole atmosphere; she regarded it as her moral duty to make the home as comfortable as possible so that the menfolk were not tempted by the sinful attractions of the outside world. Cleanliness and respectability were pursued to an almost excessive degree. Informants referring to homes kept 'as clean as snow' and everything possible being 'scrubbed white' underline their constant struggle to overcome dirt in a house where possibly two or three miners would return home, daily, covered with coal dust. To be clean was to be respectable, an important standing amongst married women.

Respectability would also be deep-rooted in a community where a very high percentage of the members were regular chapel-attenders. The middle-aged housewives of the 1920s would have experienced the aftermath of the 1904–5 religious revival. Respect for the authority of God geared them to respect not only their fellow-members but also their proud possessions. Bearing in mind the Victorian precept that cleanliness was next to godliness, being clean and houseproud was synonymous in their opinion with being respectable. The upper working-class strove to emulate the professional and middle-class sector in possessing good and fashionable pieces of furniture. Having struggled to buy these 'fetish' pieces with their husbands' hard-earned income, they would do their utmost to look after them. It is discernible from the informants' letters that table-leg covers were used by the very houseproud mothers and grandmothers, of whom many were chapel-attenders, who taught their families to respect everything in life:

> In my young days I always remember seeing the cloth around legs of furniture . . . We were a family of six boys and two sisters, all reared up with the word of respect that's missing today . . . We were a fine, great family, reared up in Chapel Life all our lives.[13]

Another informant referred to the discipline kept within the home, and remembered them being taught as children not to mark the furniture or woodwork in the house.

> Table-legs were covered and we were eight children and I don't remember one door being kicked or slammed . . . We were not allowed to kick anything, nor the furniture.[14]

Respect for valuable possessions is emphasized yet again by the informant who makes the point that 'families bought furniture to last their lifetime, money was scarce, people looked after their furniture with great care'.[15]

It is fair to deduce from this survey that, during the early decades of the twentieth century, table-leg covers were used by housewives within the Welsh industrial community primarily for protection. A supposedly Victorian custom may have been misinterpreted and given a more functional role. It was also in tune with the general trend of protecting much coveted possessions with covers, a notable characteristic of the Welsh upper-working-class home within living memory. Nicely upholstered sofas and armchairs have always been protected with loose covers, expensive squares of carpets have been covered with old rugs, and even fashionable dresses and skirts have been hidden with pinafores and

Chenille covers fitted around the legs of a table for protection at Brynaman. The custom was in practice at this house from the 1920s to 1972.

aprons. These 'covers' would be removed on very rare and special occasions. From day to day the owners deprived themselves of the pleasure of admiring the true beauty of their coveted possessions; this privilege was allowed only to the occasional visitor. The owner, on the other hand, having fulfilled the ambition of attaining these possessions, concentrated on protecting them and keeping them in pristine condition.

On the whole, the table-leg covers themselves were not regarded as items of aesthetic value. Old woollen stockings were utilized and adapted without incurring any further expense. Yet many of the informants, in their letters, emphasize that the more fashion-conscious housewife upgraded the type and quality of covers used. Many have described them as being custom-made from cretonne, chintz or damask material chosen to match the soft furnishing fabric used within the same room:

> In my aunt's house, drawstring table-leg covers were made from cretonne material to match the curtains in both kitchen and parlour. They were tied with tassels.[16]

Leg-covers of this upgraded category exceeded their basic utilitarian function; they were in tune with the artistic attributes of the housewife who concentrated on creating an attractively furnished room. The leg covers were now regarded as an integral part of the room decor. They had been given a new role. As part of the room 'display' they were to be admired in their own right. It was no longer obvious that they were concealing objects of beauty. Indeed, the overzealous effort of protecting the decorative legs finally resulted in a change of focus. The original 'objects of beauty' were gradually relegated and became inferior to the aesthetically accepted covers. This type of cover would not be removed for the benefit of visitors. In fact, they were not discarded until a new generation of 'houseproud' wives was born. As one informant, then aged 49, wrote in 1985:

> As I grew up and became houseproud, these covers were thrown out.[17]

NOTES

[1] Judi Calder, *The Victorian Home* (London, 1977), p.33.
[2] Bernard Price, *The Story of English Furniture* (1976), p.142.
[3] Calder, *The Victorian Home*, p.96.
[4] Geoffrey Warren, *A Stitch in Time* (1976), p.78.
[5] Alastair Service, *Edwardian Interiors* (London, 1982), pp.35–6.
[6] Ieuan Gwynedd Jones, 'Merthyr Tydfil in 1850', *Glamorgan Historian*, 4 (1967), 37–8.
[7] Museum of Welsh Life (hereafter MWL) tapes, nos. 7089–90, Mrs Janet Davies, Rhyd-y-car, Merthyr Tydfil.
[8] John Gloag, *Victorian Comfort* (London, 1961), p.83.

⁹ Ralph Dutton, *The Victorian Home* (London, 1954), p.88; James Laver, *Taste and Fashion* (London, 1937), p.201.

¹⁰ MWL MS 3394/13, R. Lloyd Jones, Aberavon, Port Talbot.

¹¹ Calder, *The Victorian Home*, p.33.

¹² MWL MS 3394/32, Mrs Georgina E. Thomas, Bridgend.

¹³ MWL MS 3394/1, Brynmor Davies, Blaengwynfi, Port Talbot.

¹⁴ MWL MS 3394/2, Leslie Griffiths, 27 Twynypandy, Pont-rhyd-y-fen.

¹⁵ MWL MS 3394/11, Mrs H. L. Jones, Llandysul.

¹⁶ MWL MS 3394/10, Mrs E. Jones, Bedwas Road, Caerphilly.

¹⁷ MWL MS 3394/6, Mrs Annette Holland, Blaenafon.

Knitting Stockings in Wales:
A Domestic Craft

Traditional skill in knitting stockings and its contribution to the domestic economy in most parts of rural Wales during the eighteenth and nineteenth centuries cannot be ignored. Indeed, the domestic stocking-industry was a notable feature of the economic life of many districts whereby men and children joined forces with the womenfolk to knit stockings – not only for the use of their own families but also for vending. Writing of Bala, in Merioneth, as a centre of the knitting industry, the Revd John Evans states in 1804 that 'knitting being the common employment of the neighbourhood for both sexes of all ages, even the men frequently take up the needles and assist the female, in labour, where the chief support of the family is derived'.[1] Robert Thomas (Ap Fychan) writing of Llanuwchllyn during the famine years in the early nineteenth century also related that the menfolk of the area were skilled in knitting stockings and that all the children in his family, one by one, were taught to knit so that they could earn a few pence to relieve the hardship.[2] Huw Evans, in his informative volume *Cwm Eithin (The Gorse Glen)*, writing of life in Merioneth and Denbighshire in the same period, also notes the importance of the knitting industry and testifies that the skilled fingers of mothers and daughters saved many a family from starvation. He relates the experience of a Richard Jones, Tŷ Cerrig, the son of a small farm, who recalled how his own mother kept the black famine away by knitting. She struck a bargain with her husband when, in common with most families, they were facing starvation in 1816 after a late harvest and a shortage of grain: 'I will knit,' she said. 'We have wool; if thou will card it, I'll spin'.[3] The father agreed to do the housework in addition to the work on the farm while the mother knitted. She set herself the task of knitting three full-length stockings a day.

References to the hardship suffered during the same period in other parts of the country emphasize the diligence of the womenfolk who knitted and sold stockings to help support their families. John Rees Jones, writing of Pontrhydfendigaid in Cardiganshire, reports that knitting stockings and selling them in Tregaron market was the salvation of many families that he knew well. He stressed that it was not only the wives of small farms that had to depend on this source of income; the wives of the larger farms were equally dependent on the same industry although they were reluctant to admit it.[4]

Knitting stockings had developed as a cottage industry in the highland districts of Wales by the eighteenth and nineteenth centuries, and was prevalent in the areas around specific market towns. Writing of the woollen industry in north Wales in the eighteenth century, historians have noted Llanrwst (Denbighshire) and Bala (Merioneth) as important centres for the stocking trade. Travellers passing through the towns in the eighteenth century remarked upon the presence of the industry and the markets held there every Saturday morning.[5] Tregaron, a market town in Cardiganshire, was the hub of the knitting industry in the counties of south-west Wales at the same period and it was reported that there were as many as 176 hosiers in the sub-district of Tregaron as late as the year 1851.[6] There is ample evidence to prove that this cottage industry continued to be essential to the economy of many families well into the late nineteenth and early twentieth centuries. Bob Owen, the renowned local historian of Croesor in Merioneth, writing of the industry in his locality in 1904 reports that 'about six women are able to support themselves by selling stockings of their own manufacture and every family knit for their own needs'.[7] Another local historian, J. Islan Jones, writing of Cardiganshire at the end of the nineteenth century, states that 'it was an exception to see a woman over 40 years old without knitting in her hands'.[8] Many of the women were dependent upon the knitting of stockings to earn a mean living.

THE WOOL

Sheep have been the mainstay of the economy in the hilly regions of Wales through the centuries, with the wool on their backs being as valuable as their meat in providing for the wellbeing of society. Fleeces spun into yarn and manufactured into flannels and cloths have been a source of warmth and comfort from generation to generation. An abundant supply of wool was at hand for the wives and daughters of hill farmers or tenants. Cottagers' wives and other members of the landless society however had to search for wool. One of the customs most beneficial to them was that of *gwlana* (wool-gathering). *Gwlana* is an old Welsh custom, similar to that of *lloffa* (gleaning in the fields after the corn harvest) and *blota* (the begging of flour). These customs were tolerated by society in order to provide for the poorer members. Persons were allowed to call on farmers who gave them a small quantity of their produce, according to season. This was an accepted method adopted by the rural society to provide for the less privileged before the birth of a welfare state or social security.

Mrs Elizabeth Rogers knitting stockings at Ffair-rhos, 1973.

Gwlana would take place towards the end of the shearing season. Huw Evans admits to being an eyewitness of this old custom and reports in detail:

> I saw many of the wool-gatherers on their journey. A farmer's wife worthy of the name would not be without two or three fleeces put aside for these itinerant gatherers. The labourers' wives would take to the road in groups of two or three, the leader being an experienced middle-aged lady accompanied by a younger gatherer who would be introduced by the leader at every farm. The regular or accepted gatherer would be the recipient of a generous bundle of wool, but the newly introduced had to be happy with a smaller portion.[9]

Elderly ladies alive today confirm that this method of wool-gathering was practised in specific districts at the turn of the century. An informant from Pennant in Montgomeryshire recalls how women from the village visited the farms in the neighbourhood. Their route took them along recognized paths, known to this day as *llwybrau gwlân* (woollen paths), and their 'harvest' would be packed neatly in pillowcases carried on their backs.[10] Another informant from the same area paid tribute to the farmers for assisting the poor at the beginning of the twentieth century. She remembers how her own grandmother benefited from this custom.[11]

In the counties of Cardiganshire, Carmarthenshire and Breconshire the most general custom of gathering wool was that of walking and combing the hedgerows and mountains for wool. To quote one example only, it has been reported that female parties walked from the coastal villages of New Quay, Llanarth, Llan-non and Llanrhystud in Cardiganshire towards Tregaron and then proceeded as far as the mountains above the Towy and the Irfon in the Llanwrtyd district. Each party of about six women carried with them sufficient provisions for a week or a fortnight, together with sacks for carrying the wool. Given permission by the farmer to comb the land, they were given shelter in the mountain farmhouses or in barns. The inhabitants of the mountain dwellings received the parties with joy, for at that period there was little communication between the inhabitants of the mountains and those of the plains. In the course of time a close relationship would develop between them; at the end of the day the wool-gatherers would help the farmers with the milking and other small tasks around the farmyard and would be given milk or *cawl* (broth) by their hosts, in return. In the evening they would gather around the turf fire on the hearth and relate the news of the lowland country to the interested inhabitants of the mountains.[12]

The 'right' to gather wool on the mountains was very valuable to the womenfolk. Young women-servants employed in service would make sure that the hiring conditions allowed them a free fortnight for wool-gathering.[13] The gatherers liked a severe winter, especially if it was followed by a good growing spring, for this led to the sheep shedding their wool freely. A cool, dry spell led to far less wool being found on the hedges.[14]

On the first morning after their arrival, the leader of the party allotted an area of mountain to each member and they would proceed to collect strands of wool from the bushes, rocks and so on. Having made a very early start (usually around 4 a.m.), often carrying their boots or clogs slung around their necks to save wear, they would collect from two to four pounds of wool a day. When hunger overcame them, they would congregate near a mountain stream and partake of a meal of barley bread, cheese and water. They would return to the farmhouse around 4 p.m. On a wet day they would spend the day picking and cleaning the wool. A popular stanza conveys this activity:

> Mae'n bwrw glaw allan
> Mae'n hindda'n y tŷ
> A merched Tregaron
> Yn chwalu gwlân du[15]
>
> [It is raining outside
> It is dry in the house

> And the girls of Tregaron
> Picking black wool]

At the end of the week or fortnight the party returned home laden with wool to provide for their families.

Informants in Merioneth and Cardiganshire testified how families relied on this method of wool-gathering, and that their descendants are proud owners of blankets woven from the wool gathered in this way. A specific quantity of the wool would also be spun into knitting yarn, of course. This wool would be picked and cleaned (*pigo*, *brycheuo*, *trwsio*) before it was taken to the local mill for spinning and weaving. Spinning was an important cottage-craft in Wales until the latter half of the eighteenth century but, with the mushrooming of the woollen mills, it became general practice in the nineteenth century to have the wool spun at the local mill.

Dyeing the wool for stocking yarn was another process that was carried out in the woollen mills in the nineteenth century but, as this proved rather costly, it continued to be carried out in some homes. A dye-pot was kept as a permanent fixture in most cottages. Oral evidence proved that the dyeing process did not follow a set pattern. Some households chose to dye the raw material before sending it to the mill, although the more general practice was to dye the yarn itself when returned in skein-form from the factory, but if received in spool-form the tendency was to dye the finished garment. In Cardiganshire details were given of using logwood powder, alum and sour urine to give a black dye.[16] Women and children were never seen wearing blue-grey stockings, generally known as pot-blue; they were exclusively worn by the menfolk, while the black dye was reserved for the female members of the family. Two Cardiganshire informants referred to the collecting of lichen for dyeing wool, but were not conversant with the details.

In Merioneth, on the other hand, lichen was commonly collected for dyeing wool in the home and also collected in large quantities for selling. It would be gathered by women and children and sold to merchants for 20 shillings a hundredweight. The plant was used mainly to dye military cloth.[17] Ap Fychan reports that as a child he collected it in 1816 to sell at 1½d. a pound.[18] In the home, lichen was used to give a light-brown dye. One informant from Merioneth described an ingenious method of obtaining a speckled yarn. A mixture of lichen, water and sour urine was boiled for a few hours. Then the yarn, in skein form, was securely bound at regular intervals with rush-peel. It was immersed in the dye and left to soak until the required colour was attained. The skeins were washed and dried before the rush-peel was removed. The white and brown speckled yarn was then ready for winding, This same informant explained that sour urine primarily helped to extract the dye from the lichen and also that stockings made from yarn treated with lichen would not draw the feet.[19]

By the nineteenth century it was also possible to buy knitting yarn from local mills, in its natural colour or dyed, blue-grey being the most common colour.

ANCILLARY OBJECTS

Having acquired a supply of knitting yarn, as skeins or spools, members of the household would proceed to wind it into balls, ready for use. Some families would provide a three-armed wooden frame – *car dirwyn* (winding-frame), custom-made to hold the skeins. Spools could also be fitted on one arm of this same frame. Otherwise, one partner would hold the skein with outstretched arms while the other partner wound it into a ball. These balls were then stored in special net-bags and kept in a dry, convenient spot.

It was general custom to wind the yarn around a small piece of folded paper to give the ball a firm foundation, but in specific parts of Carmarthenshire, Cardiganshire, Merioneth and Denbighshire, a special device was used for this purpose. On killing a goose at Christmas-time its windpipe would be cleaned and, while supple, it would be filled with very small stones and then turned to make a perfect circle. It was then allowed to dry before use as a foundation for a ball of knitting yarn. When knitting by candlelight, the ball would be placed in a custom-made holder on the floor but, if it happened to roll on the floor, the rattle of the stones would help to locate it.[20]

Yarn hooks were commonly used by knitters throughout the country, more especially when they were knitting while walking. In the shape of an elaborate 'S', one hook would be attached to the apron waistband or string while the ball would be suspended from the lower hook. These yarn hooks would vary in quality and design and were often presented as love-tokens. In the Museum of Welsh Life collection there is a wide variety made of brass, copper and other metals. Some bear the initials of the recipient, others include heart-shaped decorations and intricate designs.

Knitters in specific districts were also the proud owners of knitting sheaths. They were regularly used by knitters in the counties of south and west Wales at the beginning of the century, but informants from Merioneth were not able to recall their being in use there, nor did they have any recollection of their mothers referring to them. The sheath (*gwain*), tucked into the strings of the apron, was usually worn on the right hip, those of scimitar-shape taking the form of the body. The right needle was placed into the bore, and the right hand, thus freed of supporting the needle, was placed close up over the needle point, the forefinger acting as a shuttle, making the least possible movement and attaining a speed of some two hundred stitches a minute. Cardiganshire knitters stressed that the sheath assisted them to knit while walking; it supported the weight of the garment and kept the needle firm to ensure even knitting. They did not always refer to the speed attained by using it. These knitting sheaths were also given as love-tokens and were adorned with fine decorations.

The lack of transport facilities in rural Wales at this period forced people to walk long distances regularly, and they seized on this opportunity to knit on their way. John Evans describes the inhabitants of the Bala district at the beginning of the nineteenth century – 'you see none idle, going out or returning home, riding or walking, they are occupied in this portable employment'.[21] This description was also true of other areas in Merioneth as well as Caernarfonshire and Cardiganshire at the turn of the twentieth century. Informants recall how their mothers and aunts would knit while carrying fodder to the cattle, knit while walking to the turbary to dig peat, knit on horseback and knit while carrying heavy baskets to market. They were also known to knit on their way to chapel meetings during the week, but the clicking of needles ceased outside the chapel gate, before they trod on sacred ground![22]

KNITTING ASSEMBLIES

The hub of the industry, however, was the hearth, where work was combined with leisure and members of a household would spend the evenings knitting during the winter months. The *noson weu* (knitting assembly) was an important social occasion in rural Wales in the eighteenth and early nineteenth centuries. Friends and neighbours would arrange to meet in one particular home to knit. Thomas Pennant witnessed such a gathering in Bala in 1747:

> During the long winter nights the females through love of society, often assemble at one another's house, to knit, sit around a fire and listen to some old tale or to some antient song or the sound of a harp – this is called *Cymmorth Gwau* or the Knitting Assembly.[23]

Carrying out a certain task in a group, on one hearth, to the accompaniment of traditional entertainment was characteristic of rural society in Wales at this period. Similar gatherings were known as *noson bilio* (rush-peeling night) and *noson bluo* (feathering night). The tasks were all important for the well-being and livelihood of the participants; they would assist one another to complete them 'while tales of other times beguile the hours or the village harper thrums his dulcet tones of harmony'.[24]

Ap Fychan, reminiscing about knitting assemblies at Llanuwchllyn at the beginning of the nineteenth century, refers to the religious tone of the conversation that took place during these sessions. The religious revivalists of the eighteenth century seem to have realized the potential of this informal and homely type of evening for their purposes. Ap Fychan has left us detailed descriptions of these meetings which prove that religion was of great concern and entertainment for the people of the Llanuwchllyn district at that time. These prearranged knitting nights lasted about three hours and were broken up at about 9 o'clock. The house where the meeting took place, the night and the topics to be discussed were generally predetermined, so that it was not held when other religious meetings took place at the local chapel or at any other venue nearby. The writer witnessed many of these meetings and he notes:

> it was the intention of the religious people of the place that these meetings should be used to good purpose and that nothing depraved should be brought into them. Topics such as these were discussed there: original sin, the influence of the Holy Ghost, justification, the sacrifice of Christ etc.[25]

Towards the end of the nineteenth century, however, the popularity of the *noson weu* in the counties of Merioneth and Denbighshire was waning. Huw Evans again gives us a vivid description of one of the last meetings he witnessed in his home area. He compares this particular type of evening during the latter half of the nineteenth century with an 'At Home' night of the twentieth century. There is no reference to the religious aspect and the emphasis is obviously on good food and jollification – a purely secular gathering. He writes:

> When it was settled to have a *noswaith weu*, the first step was to decide whom to invite, the number of course depending upon the size of the house and the host's resources. On the day, the housewife would be kept busy all afternoon baking lightcakes, griddlecakes and packing the children off to the village to buy a white loaf and a pound of loaf sugar. The guests were usually young people – both male and female. The girls arrived first, and it was considered to be the proper thing for the young men to linger a little before putting in an appearance. When all had arrived, the womenfolk would begin to knit and one or two lads – inveterate jokers – would also produce needles and yarn and begin to knit garters. To tell the truth, there was not much solid work done at a *noswaith weu* as so much time was spent in laughing at stories and picking up stitches after the lads had pulled out the needles.[26]

A good storyteller was always in great demand for these occasions and some of them had a great store of tales of the *tylwyth teg* (the fairies) and other folk tales. Their purpose was twofold: they amused the company and they caused female members to be far too nervous of walking home without a male escort! At these gatherings song and story were focal, and the *noson weu* was instrumental in preserving these traditional forms of folklore.

The knitting assemblies of the early nineteenth century in the counties of south-west Wales had yet another distinctive characteristic. John Evans notes this distinction:

> The custom was observed in north Wales of meeting in each other's houses for a view of sociality – here economy is observed. They frequently knit what they call *guird* for no other wager hut honour. They let loose from bottoms of balls equal lengths of yarn tied together and the first that knits up to the knot becomes the conqueror and receives the praise. This emulation tends to give them a great facility and quickness in the use of needles.[27]

We have an account of such a competitive evening held in the Llanwrtyd area at the end of the nineteenth century. The gathering, known as *gweu-dechreunos* (early-evening knitting), would be arranged and some six or more female knitters would be invited to attend. Male friends would also be asked to be present and one of them would be elected to promote the competition. He would measure, for each competitor, one fathom (i.e. a *gwryd*) from the last point of knitting and mark this length with a knot. All competitors were given a signal to start knitting this length simultaneously, and the one to complete it in the shortest time was the champion of the evening.[28] One informant in the Bronnant district of north Cardiganshire, who was ninety-four years old in 1978, remembers such a meeting being held in her home when she was a young girl. The meeting was known there as *gweu gwryd* and she confirmed that the aim of such a competition was to promote or accelerate the knitting.[29]

TYPE OF STOCKINGS

Stockings produced for the markets were usually knitted in plain stocking-stitch with a ribbed welt. Indeed some knitters were accused of using inferior wool for this purpose and also of knitting them too loosely in order to conserve wool. However it was regular practice in Cardiganshire to knit the welt and toe in natural white yarn while the bulk of the stocking would he knitted in the blue-grey dyed yarn. Some informants stressed that the natural colour yarn wore better than the dyed one and therefore was more suitable for the toe-caps.[30] A scientific reason given for knitting the welt and toe-caps in natural colour yarn was that the oil or lanolin present in it gave added warmth and protection to the wearer's toes. The oil would also weatherproof the welts of the stockings which were often exposed to the weather when worn above the tops of boots: they would thus readily shed any moisture.[31] However, when knitting for the family, it was the general custom in most areas to knit the stockings in a ribbed pattern (*sane brogs* or *sane rips*). Ribbed stockings would cling to the leg and thus gave the wearer better protection. A more ambitious pattern would be that of a cable stitch (*patrwm rhaff* or *patrwm igam-ogam*; 'rope pattern' or 'zig-zag pattern').

To knit an ornamental pattern on the side of the stocking is a well-known tradition in both England and Wales. William Salesbury in a sixteenth-century Welsh manuscript refers to 'cwyrk hosan a clocke' (a stocking quirk with clocks).[32] The definition of the English term *quirk* in the *Oxford English Dictionary* in relation to stockings is 'a clock, an ornamental pattern in silk worked on the side of a stocking'. From this English term *quirk* developed a Welsh verbnoun *cwirco* with the meaning 'to make a pattern or a quirk on stockings'. Thomas Edwards (Twm o'r Nant) wrote the following line in the eighteenth century when describing the costume of an old colourful character: 'Sgidiau pingc a hosanau cwirciau' (Pink shoes and quirked stockings).[33] Gradually, the term quirk was loosely applied to any pattern knitted into one or both sides of the stocking as opposed to the silk pattern worked on them. When taking specific knitting orders from customers, a local, established knitter would usually enquire: 'What kind of quirk would you like on your stocking?' It could be a cable or a definite rib-stitch on both sides. When wearing low shoes without leggings a man would be proud to show his quirked stockings.[34]

Having been knitted at every possible opportunity the completed garments were pressed beneath stocking boards (*styllod sanau*) and were then ready for the market. These boards were cut to the shape of a stocking and informants from Cardiganshire described how a pile of stockings would be positioned between two boards which were then pressed by the weight of a heavy stone resting on the upper board for a whole week. Another method practised in north Wales was that of placing a preheated board inside the stockings.

STOCKING MARKETS

It has been recorded that Welsh cattle-drovers of the eighteenth century took stockings with them to sell in English market towns. It has also been reported that the knitters of Trawsfynydd, Merioneth, frequently congregated on the route of the stagecoach offering their stockings for sale to travellers, and there were still wayside knitters at Pentrefoelas (Denbighshire) on the Holyhead road in Borrow's time,[35] but the general pattern in the nineteenth century was to take them to sell at the local market or fair. Reaching the market from remote farms was no mean feat for the womenfolk and it often meant a walk of some twenty miles to complete the journey, carrying their bundles of stockings in sacks over their backs on their outward journey and replacing them for the return journey with provisions bought with the proceeds.

In the counties of north Wales the two most notable stocking fairs were those held weekly in Llanrwst and Bala. Of Llanrwst market, it was reported by R. Fenton (1814) that £300 worth of stockings were sold in the morning before the market began by the knitters themselves.[36] Elizabeth Williams in her autobiography *Siaced Fraith* remembers her own grandmother at the beginning of the twentieth century attending this fair every week to sell her stockings to the stocking man.[37]

However, Bala was the most important centre for the stocking trade in the counties of north Wales in the eighteenth and nineteenth centuries. In 1748, the weekly value of the stockings sold was £200 and the sale of knitted articles at Bala accounted for one-fifth (£10,000) of the estimated woollen manufactures of Merioneth.[38] The industry grew in importance later in the century. Pennant estimated the weekly value of the sales at Bala as £500 in 1780,[39] while at the turn of the century it was estimated that 200,000 pairs of stockings (worth £18,000) were disposed of in one year – selling at an average price of between a 1s. 4d. and five shillings a pair, and children's socks at eightpence a pair. The industry continued to thrive during the early part of the nineteenth century. By 1830, 32,000 dozen pairs of knit worsted stockings were sold annually in Bala, 10,000 dozen pairs of socks and 5,500 dozen pairs of woollen gloves.[40] The decline of the industry came later in the century with the competition from factory-made hose from the English Midlands which was facilitated by the advent of the railway. In the 1851 census, only 105 people in north Wales described themselves as 'knitters' and another 148 as 'stocking manufacturers'.

In the counties of south Wales, there are records of small stocking-fairs being held in the eighteenth century in Llantwit Major, Llandaf and Caerphilly in Glamorgan,[41] and in Llanybydder, Llandovery and Llangamarch in Carmarthenshire and Breconshire.[42] At Llantwit Major, for example, cotton and yarn stockings and Welsh wigs were manufactured and sold at the monthly markets. John Franklin of Llanfihangel near Cowbridge, established the March fair at Cowbridge, called Franklin's Fair, 'to provide farmers with some means of raising money to pay their Lady Day rents', by selling the products of the spare-time knitting.[43] The main centre of trade for the south-west Wales counties in the eighteenth and nineteenth centuries, second only in importance to that of Bala, was Tregaron in Cardiganshire. The takings for stocking sales in Tregaron in the early 1800s averaged £40 a week – the stockings varying in price from 6s. to £6 a dozen pairs, that is, 6d. to 10s. 6d. a pair, most of them being sold at 8d. a pair.[44] At the end of the nineteenth century, the average weekly sum taken for stockings at Tregaron is given as £200.[45] Informants whose mothers had sold stockings at this fair at this period reported that the average price given by the hosiers for a well-knitted pair was 2s. 6d. or 3s., although the hosiers were reluctant to pay this sum and were too ready to find flaws in the knitting and were even known to push a finger through a weak stitch in order to lower the price![46]

In his report on agriculture and domestic economy of both north and south Wales, 1810–15, Walter Davies (Gwallter Mechain) gives a breakdown of the cost of knitting a pair of stockings. Having stated that a woman may card, spin and knit four pairs of stockings per week, he writes:

> one pair of these stockings weighs near half a pound, which at 10d. a pound is 5d. out of the 8d. for which they are sold in the market [Tregaron] – but the price has since advanced . . . we may fairly state the raw materials of each pair of stockings to be worth 5d. – hence the woman has only 3d. for carding, spinning and knitting a pair of these stockings or 1s. a week. Hence the woman has to support herself in food, raiment, fuel and house rent, for seven days upon this 1s., yet at some times of the year it will buy her only *one gallon of wheat*. Such is the employment and such the only means of subsistence within reach of the poorer sort of females all over this extensive tract, although these are as remarkable for industry as the males are for an aversion to labour.[47]

He draws a similar conclusion about the industry in the counties of north Wales, where, he reports:

> the profit of manufacture is a *mere trifle* and would never answer, were not the knitting of such the occupation of their leisure hours, in walking or by the fireside on a long winter's night – without expense of candle and the means of instructing children.[48]

He pointed out that the industry could not hope to survive unless a factory for knitting be set up in the Bala area. However, he was proved wrong; stocking manufacturing remained a domestic craft to the end, and oral evidence gained from informants in this area proves that this 'mere trifle' was an essential contribution to the domestic economy of the highland districts of Wales until the turn of the twentieth century.

STOCKING MEN OR HOSIERS

We must finally consider the role of the stocking men or hosiers as they were known (*dynion sane, porthmon sane*), who bought the bulk at the fairs and sold them to the consumers. The 'Welsh hosiers' who attended Bala fair were mostly Englishmen employed by merchants from Shrewsbury and elsewhere to buy stockings for resale in London and other English towns, supplying shops and warehouses.[49] However, it is known that local men became agents, one of the most prosperous of them being Gabriel Davies, described in a trade directory of 1815 as 'Grocer, Draper and Welsh woollen yarn, hosiery and flannel merchant'. He is the person described by Fenton as 'the great stocking merchant at Bala . . . who died worth half a million'.[50] Bob Owen recorded references to thirty-one local hosiery merchants active in Merioneth between 1690 and 1925.[51] References to three local agents in the Bala district in the early 1820s were found in a general merchant's account book from this area. Customers' accounts were entered under their names, description of trade or employment, and address:

1824	John Nannau, Hosier, Tyddynmercher	
1823–8	Thomas Davies, Hosier, Llangower	
1827	John Rowlands, Hosier, Bwlchybuarth.[52]	

Both English and Welsh hosiers were also involved in the stocking trade in Glamorgan in the late seventeenth and early eighteenth centuries. They bought the stockings from local inhabitants at the local fairs and markets and sold them to customers in the west of England. It has been recorded that a large number of 'fardels' (bundles) and 'bags' of stockings were regularly exported from the small ports of Cardiff, Sully, Aberthaw and Newton to Bristol and Minehead.[53] For example, of the forty-two shipments despatched from Cardiff to Bristol in 1666, twenty-two included various quantities of stockings. The extent of the Glamorgan stocking-trade may be partly assessed from the following table, which shows the total number of bags and fardels of stockings exported from Aberthaw and Newton to Bristol and Minehead for the years stated, and as indicated in the official port books.[54]

Year	Total no. bags and fardels of stockings	Approximate no. of pairs
1667	73	8989
1670	90	11070
1672	103	12669
1674	115	13795
1678	97	11736
1680	124	15752
1683	351	50193
1685	139	19877
1686	92	13156
1688	186	26598
1689	108 (+100 dozen)	16044
1692	57 (+ 30 dozen)	8181
1694	75	10725
1695	129	18447
1696	92	13156
1697	66	9438
1698	70	10010
1699	49 (July–Dec. only)	7007
1701	70	10010

Probate inventories of various Glamorgan men show that they were evidently acting as hosiers at this period. The probate inventory of Richard John of St George's shows that he owned 'A packe of stokins' worth £10. Likewise, the 'goods and chattells' of John Bomand, a weaver of St Bride's Major, included a 'parcel of stockings' (valued at £5) and that of Thomas William, a gentleman of Llanwynno, 'six dozen women's stockings' (valued at £1 8s. 0d.). Similar records show that local people traded directly with English hosiers who must have visited specific parts of Glamorgan at this period. We find that Edward Marcus, Thomas Chrichard, John Pinch and Christopher Pike, all hosiers of 'ye City of Exon', were debtors to Margaret Roberts, widow of Llanharry, who, in 1696, made one bequest to her son of 'ten pounds sterling which is due to me from Edward Marcus, a hosier in ye citty of Exon'.[55]

In the Tregaron district of Cardiganshire, however, it seems that, by the nineteenth century, local personalities anxious to find a source of income became itinerant pedlars of stockings. They bought their supplies of stockings in the local market and then proceeded to carry them to the industrial towns of south Wales where they found a ready market for them. We have references

A 'stocking man' from Llanwrtyd, taken in 1905 at the request of Sir John Ballinger (then Cardiff City Librarian). According to Ballinger's notes, he 'lives in Llanwrtyd and travels the country round to markets & fairs. He can be met in Builth, Erwood, Talgarth, Brecon and similar places regularly . . . His business is as a vendor only, he is not a maker – he buys from the makers around Llanwrtyd.'

(both from documented and oral sources) to two such personalities from the Bronnant district of Tregaron, namely Morgan Parry, from Rhos-y-wlad, Bronnant, who eventually became a well-known drover and farmer, and a Thomas George (Tomos Siors).[56] The weekly route taken by this one hosier

The stone commemorating John Caron Morgan (John Sana) in the graveyard of St Michael's Church, Cwmafan. He died in 1923, aged 81.

from Tregaron to Merthyr in the latter half of the nineteenth century has been recorded by two local historians.[57] The focal point of the stocking trade in Tregaron was the inn situated in the main square, aptly known as the Hosiers Arms. Having attended the fair there on a Tuesday, Tomos Siors would then proceed on his journey over the mountain towards Abergwesyn (twelve miles), attending a smaller fair there, and then onward to Llanwrtyd Wells (four miles) and another trade-centre in the home of one Cati Dafis, where he stayed overnight. On the following day he would continue over the Epynt Mountain to Brecon (twelve miles as the crow flies), and on the third day he would complete the journey from Brecon to Merthyr over the Brecon Beacons. He would have to face the return journey, again on foot, in time to attend the Tregaron fair on the following Tuesday. A well-known Welsh poet, J. T. Thomas (Sarnicol), has also recorded this itinerary in metric stanzas, naming the ports of call en route – Grouse Inn, Abergwesyn, and the Storey Arms on the Brecon Beacons.[58] Of Merthyr he writes:

> Gwisgwyr sane'r greadigaeth
> A ddaw yna 'nghyd
> Sane glas a gwyn y Cardi
> Geir ar goesau'r byd.

> [Stocking wearers of all creation
> Here are found
> The blue and white stockings of the Cardi
> On the world's legs abound.]

Marie Trevelyan refers to the itinerant Welsh hosiers' round in the industrial valleys of Glamorgan at the end of the nineteenth century. She writes of their significant role in the mining community:

> next in importance to the packmen were the stocking-sellers and flannel weavers. They are generally grave solemn-looking persons, very respectful in their manners, and as a rule, they speak a little imperfect English. They, unlike the packmen, are not great talkers, but careful and strictly honest vendors of their wares.[59]

She describes their method of carrying their stock – suspended from special frames resting on their shoulders. Two informants from Pont-rhyd-y-fen,

Glamorgan, remember one such itinerant pedlar, John Morgan (known locally as John Sana) in their village at the turn of the twentieth century. They described the frame as being of a very simple construction and it was known as *ors sana* (stocking horse).[60]

It is recorded that with the advent of the railway in 1866 the itinerant pedlar of south-west Wales gradually changed his image by becoming a market-stall holder and eventually a shopkeeper in the main market towns of south Wales. Having set up a permanent stall or woollen shop in Glamorgan, he now depended on members of his family in the Tregaron area to act as agents for him, forwarding the hosiery and flannel to him by rail. With the decline of the trade later in the century, the hosier's shop became a more general draper's store with the whole family migrating to the coalfield district.[61] Through oral evidence it has been possible to trace the story of one John Edwards of Tregaron, an itinerant hosier who sold stockings from door to door in the mining villages of Aberdare, Maerdy and Ferndale; but in the later years of the nineteenth century he was able to open a woollen shop, namely Albion House, in the village of Pentre in the Rhondda valley. A lady informant, who was employed in this shop in the early 1920s, revealed that the trade, at this period, was centred mainly around Welsh flannel items – for example, flannel shirts and drawers – and Welsh tweeds, but home-knitted stockings and stocking yarn were still available although the demand for them had markedly decreased.[62]

With the development of the woollen industry and the advent of the railways, factory-produced machine-made stockings were brought to the village shops of north Wales in the early decades of the twentieth century and the cottage industry gradually declined. Similarly, in the counties of south and west Wales, the introduction of knitted goods produced by the hosiery manufacturers of the east Midlands, Scotland and north of England had a detrimental effect on the demand for hand-knitted hose, and consequently the domestic craft in all its aspects ceased.

NOTES

[1] Revd John Evans, *Letters Written During a Tour Through North Wales* (London, 1804), p.88.
[2] W. Lliedi Williams, *Hunangofiant ac Ysgrifau Ap Fychan* (Caerdydd, 1948), pp.11, 34 (trans.).
[3] Huw Evans, *The Gorse Glen* (Liverpool, 1948), pp.14–15.
[4] John Rees Jones, *Sôn am y Bont* (Llandysul, 1974), p.73 (trans.).
[5] T. Pennant, *Tours in Wales* (1810), II, p.210; R. Fenton, *Tours in Wales* (1804–13), Appendix III, p.313.
[6] Emrys Jones, 'Tregaron' in Elwyn Davies and Alwyn D. Rees, ed., *Welsh Rural Communities* (Cardiff, 1962), pp.74–5.

7   Bob Owen, *Diwydiannau Coll* (Lerpwl, 1943), p.65 (trans.).

8   J. Islan Jones, *Yr Hen Amser Gynt* (Aberystwyth, 1958), pp.81–2 (trans.).

9   Huw Evans, *The Gorse Glen*, p.171.

10 Museum of Welsh Life (hereafter MWL) tape, no. 3463, Mrs Mary Davies, Pennant, Llanbryn-mair.

11 MWL tape, no. 3465, Mrs Mari Lewis, Bont Dolgadfan, Llanbryn-mair.

12 MWL MS 1793/399, Mr Evan Jones, Ty'n-y-pant, Llanwrtyd.

13 Ibid.

14 W. J. Lewis, 'Labour in mid-Cardiganshire in the early nineteenth century', *Ceredigion*, 4 (1963), 330–1.

15 MWL MS 1793/399, Mr Evan Jones.

16 MWL tape, no. 3841, Mrs Mary Jenkins, Ffair-rhos.

17 Lewis, 'Labour in mid-Cardiganshire in the early nineteenth century', 331.

18 Williams, *Hunangofiant ac Ysgrifau Ap Fychan*, p.12.

19 MWL tape, no. 5142, Mrs Sarah Davies, Y Bala.

20 MWL MS 1793/483, Mr Evan Jones; oral testimony, Mrs Elin Jane Edwards, Llanuwchllyn, and Mrs M. Parry, Dyffryn Ceiriog.

21 Evans, *Letters Written During a Tour Through North Wales*, p.88.

22 MWL tape, no. 5138, Mrs Sara Elin Roberts, Y Bala; MWL tape, no. 5135, Mr Elis Davies, Llanuwchllyn; oral testimony, Mrs Mari James, Llangeitho, and Miss Cassie Davies, Tregaron.

23 Pennant, *Tours in Wales*, p.211.

24 Evans, *Letters Written During a Tour Through North Wales*, p.88.

25 Robert Thomas (Ap Fychan) in *Y Dyddiau Gynt* in *Y Dysgedydd* (1867), trans. by T. M. Owen, in *Welsh Rural Communities*, p.210.

26 Huw Evans, *The Gorse Glen*, pp.147–8.

27 Revd John Evans, *Letters Written During a Tour Through South Wales* (London, 1804), pp.357–8.

28 MWL MS 1793/312, Mr Evan Jones.

29 MWL tape, no. 4980, Mrs Margaret Morgan, Bronnant, Cards.

30 MWL tape, no. 4973, Mrs Elizabeth Rogers, Ffair-rhos.

31 Oral testimony, Miss P. Davies, Church Stretton, Salop.

32 William Salesbury, *A Dictionary in Englishe and Welshe* (1547; reprint 1877).

33 Twm o'r Nant, *Y Ddau Ben Ymdrechgar, sef Cyfoeth a Thylodi etc.* (1780, 1841).

34 MWL MS 1793/334, Mr Evan Jones.

35 J. Geraint Jenkins, *The Welsh Woollen Industry* (Cardiff, 1969), p.212.

36 Fenton, *Tours in Wales*, p.313.

37 Elizabeth Williams, *Siaced Fraith* (Aberystwyth, 1952), p.45.

38 M. J. Jones, 'The woollen industry of Merioneth, 1758–1820', *Transactions of the Honourable Society of Cymmrodorion* (1939), 199.

39 Ibid.

40 *Municipal Corporations Report* (1837–8), vol. 35, p.229 (quoted by M. J. Jones, 'The woollen industry of Merioneth').

41 Jenkins, *The Welsh Woollen Industry*, p.312.

42 Walter Davies, *General View of the Agriculture and Domestic Economy of South Wales*, vol. 2 (London, 1815), pp.438–44, 487–9.

43 Cardiff City Library, Cadrawd MS 2.355.

44 Lewis, 'Labour in mid-Cardiganshire in the early nineteenth century', 331.

45 Evan Jones, *Cerdded Hen Ffeiriau* (Aberystwyth, 1972), pp.34, 35.

46 MWL tapes, nos. 4975–6, Mrs E. Ebenezer, Llangeitho; MWL tape, no. 4982, Miss E. Morgan, Bronnant.

47 Walter Davies, *General View of the Agriculture and Domestic Economy of South Wales*, pp.442–3.

48 Walter Davies, *General View of the Agriculture and Domestic Economy of North Wales* (London, 1813), pp.404–5.

49 Jenkins, *The Welsh Woollen Industry*, p.212.

50 Fenton, *Tours in Wales*, p.123.

51 Bob Owen, 'Hanes y diwydiant gwlân yn Sir Feirionnydd' (1950), National Library of Wales MS 19271, p.101, quoted in Jenkins, *The Welsh Woollen Industry*, pp.213–14.

52 MS Z/DS/A/116, Area Record Office, Dolgellau.

53 Moelwyn I. Williams, *The Economic and Social History of Glamorgan*, Glamorgan County History, vol. IV (1974), p.342.

54 Ibid., p.243, taken from Public Records Office, E190/1277/7.

55 Moelwyn I. Williams, *The Economic and Social History of Glamorgan*, pp.342–3, taken from National Library of Wales, PR (Ll.), 1674; 1696; 1722–3; 1714.

56 Evan Jones, *Cerdded Hen Ffeiriau*, pp.35, 37; MWL tape, no. 3841, Mrs Mary Jenkins.

57 Evan Jones, *Cerdded Hen Ffeiriau*; MWL MS 1793/38, Mr Evan Jones, Ty'n-y-pant, Llanwrtyd.

58 Evan Jones, *Cerdded Hen Ffeiriau*, pp.37–9.

59 Marie Trevelyan, *Glimpses of Welsh Life and Character* (London, 1893), pp.24–5.

60 Oral testimony, Mrs Sarah Jane Evans, Pont-rhyd-y-fen, and Miss Mary Harcombe, Cwmafan, Pont-rhyd-y-fen.

61 Emrys Jones, 'Tregaron', pp.74–5.

62 Oral testimony, Mrs May Samuel, Treorci.

Index